KNOW
YOUR
POWER

KNOW
YOUR
POWER

A Message to America's Daughters

NANCY PELOSI

with Amy Hill Hearth

DOUBLEDAY

NEW YORK   LONDON   TORONTO   SYDNEY   AUCKLAND

ꓷꓷ

DOUBLEDAY

Published in the United States by Doubleday,
an imprint of The Doubleday Publishing Group,
a division of Random House, Inc., New York.
www.doubleday.com

DOUBLEDAY is a registered trademark and the DD colophon
is a trademark of Random House, Inc.

Book design by Chris Welch

Library of Congress Cataloging-in-Publication Data
Pelosi, Nancy, 1940–
Know your power : a message to America's daughters / by Nancy Pelosi with
Amy Hill Hearth.—1st ed.
p. cm.
1. Pelosi, Nancy, 1940– 2. Women politicians—United States—Biography.
3. Women in politics—United States—History. I. Hearth, Amy Hill, 1958–
II. Title.
HQ1391.U5P45 2008
328.73092—dc22
[B]
2008020607

ISBN 978-0-385-52586-2

PRINTED IN THE UNITED STATES OF AMERICA

1 3 5 7 9 10 8 6 4 2

First Edition

To Paul a/k/a Daddy a/k/a Pop
a wonderful husband, father, and grandfather

CONTENTS

Acknowledgments ix

Preface 1

PART ONE
ROOTS AND WINGS

1 Never Lose Faith 5

2 Declarations of Independence 9

3 An Open House 21

4 Love Happens 31

5 Be Open to the New 45

PART TWO
KITCHEN TO CONGRESS

6 Recognize Opportunity 61

CONTENTS

7 *Organize, Don't Agonize* 69

8 *A Voice That Will Be Heard* 87

9 *"Age Quod Agis": Do What You Are Doing* 99

10 *Think Outside the Beltway* 109

PART THREE
KNOW YOUR POWER

11 *A Seat at the Table* 123

12 *There Is No Secret Sauce* 131

13 *Remember When You Used to Cook?* 141

14 *The Qualities You Need* 147

15 *The Speaker and the President* 155

16 *What Matters Most* 165

Index 175

ACKNOWLEDGMENTS

Notes, Notes, Take Notes! That was the advice that Norman Brokaw, the Chairman of William Morris Agency, had been giving me for years—ever since I met him at lunch with my friend Roz Wyman. When I became House Democratic Whip and then Leader he became even more insistent. I never took the time to take notes, but when I became Speaker, Norman said—Notes or not, it's time to write the book. And so my first acknowledgment is to Norman for our long friendship and his cheerful guidance.

I am deeply in Norman's debt for his introduction to his associate, Mel Berger, who held my feet to the fire, my pen to the pad, and my message on point. I am grateful to

Mel for his constant attention, his wordsmithing, and his candor. Mel became my taskmaster, my editor, and my friend.

I appreciated hearing the perspective of Jennifer Rudolph Walsh, a William Morris Agency executive. As a successful dynamic working mother of young children, Jennifer's views were especially important to me.

How proud I am to have *Know Your Power* published by Doubleday under the masterful direction of Phyllis Grann. I am grateful to Phyllis and her associates at Doubleday for their expert advice, counsel, and editing.

Thanks also to James Kaplan, who patiently got us off to a good start with his interviews of my family, including my brothers Thomas and Nicholas; my political and personal friends John Burton and Willie Brown about San Francisco politics; Chairman George Miller and Congresswoman Anna Eshoo about the U.S. Congress; Rita Murray Meyer about Trinity College, and Judy Lemons about the Presidio.

Heeding Phyllis's sage admonition that the book should not be a thousand pages long, Amy Hill Hearth helped make the book more succinct. I loved working with her and hearing her wisdom about what to cut and what to keep. And what we kept was greatly enhanced by Amy's craftsmanship.

Personally, I am most grateful to the D'Alesandro family—my parents and brothers and especially my mother—for loving me so much. And to my own family, for making my life so fulfilled, and for making my roles as wife, mother, and grandmother my proudest credentials to become the first woman Speaker of the House.

That is the message I want America's daughters to take note of—for themselves and their daughters.

Preface

On the fourth of January, 2007, I was sworn in as the first woman Speaker of the House of Representatives in U.S. history, the highest elected office any woman had achieved.

Becoming the Speaker is a significant accomplishment, but I have never felt it was a personal victory. Rather, I see it as a pivotal moment for all women.

When I became Speaker, it was *American women* who made history that day.

I didn't set out to be Speaker of the House. But throughout my life, there were openings, opportunities, and choices that brought me to this time and place.

With this book, I hope to share my story and the lessons

I have learned along the way, the ones that other women generously shared with me, enabling my path to power. Others are lessons taught to me by my parents, or learned as a wife to a remarkable man, as a mother of five, and now as a grandmother of seven. In this book, the personal and the professional overlap as they so often do in life.

I find it humbling and deeply moving when women and girls approach me looking for insight and advice. It is my intention, in the pages of this book, to answer their questions in a way that I hope is both inspiring and practical, as if I were speaking to all of America's daughters, simply telling them about myself, what I believe, and what others have taught me along the way.

Raising a family is challenging. I want women to know that the skills I acquired as a mother and homemaker have been invaluable to me. These same skills—so often undervalued—are transferable to many other arenas in life, including the United States Congress.

If women can learn from me, in the same way I learned from the women who came before me, it will make the honor of being Speaker of the House even greater. May the examples I share from my life help others to know their power.

Nancy Pelosi

Washington, D.C.

PART ONE

ROOTS AND WINGS

1

I t was a cold day in January 1987 when I said goodbye to Sala. I didn't know it at the time—or perhaps I simply wasn't ready to accept it—but my friend was dying.

Sala Burton was a Congresswoman from California whom I had known, along with her late husband, Phillip, for many years. She was one of the women I admired most, as well as a close friend.

Everyone respected Sala and knew not to underestimate her. She looked like Mother Earth; she spoke with a Polish accent; she didn't drive a car. She gave off an intense warmth—if she liked you. She was passionate about what she believed in, but very dispassionate about her politics.

Sala was like family to me. She loved my children and was especially close to my two oldest daughters, Nancy Corinne and Christine. Nancy Corinne started at Mount Vernon College in Washington shortly after Sala went to Congress, and called us one day to say that she needed a car.

"Why do you think you should have a car in college?" my husband, Paul, and I asked. With five children, providing each one with a car in college was not in the budget. "I need a car for Sala," Nancy Corinne said. "I have to drive Sala around."

So we sent our old Jeep Wrangler from San Francisco. It was quite a sight to see Nancy Corinne driving the dignified Sala Burton around Washington in a car with removable windows.

A couple of years later, Sala became ill with cancer. We thought she could win any battle. But this was one she could not.

And so the time came to say goodbye. Anyone who has ever visited a friend who is dying will know how hard it is. What was astonishing to me, however, was her self-lessness. Despite my protests, what she wanted most to talk about was me.

A circle of her friends, whom she had summoned, gathered around her bed. Solemnly she announced the sad news: She would not be seeking reelection because she was very ill. She then turned to me and asked me to run for her seat. She wanted me to accept her endorsement on the spot.

"Sala, please don't talk this way," I said. "You're breaking my heart."

I still held out hope that she would get better. Finally she convinced me that my agreement was the only answer that would bring her comfort, and so, with great sadness, I promised I would run for Congress.

I often look back on that day in wonder.

We all admired Sala's strength and grace, but what was striking was the faith she had in me. Sometimes it takes the encouragement of someone who knows us well to propel us forward in ways we never would have dreamed. I was confident in my abilities and accomplishments, but Sala's faith in me was so unshakable that it made me determined to live up to it.

And so I ran for Congress—and won. I was forty-seven years old, a mother of five, happily married, and never—not even once—thinking or wanting this to happen to me.

In the campaign, I had to face many challenges. Like many women, I was hesitant to talk about myself and my achievements, but I became much more at ease because I believed deeply in everything I said about the issues.

What lifts you up, what helps you to grow, is the excitement of the people around you. When I announced my candidacy in mid-February that year, I walked into the ILWU union hall expecting to see a few friends and reporters; instead, there was a large, enthusiastic crowd. Their support made me determined to win, not just for myself but for all of them.

Twenty years later, as I was sworn in as the first woman Speaker of the House, faith again was very much on my mind. I thought of all the women throughout American history who'd had faith that one day we would achieve equality with men.

As I accepted the gavel from Republican Leader John Boehner, I told my colleagues:

"This is an historic moment—for the Congress, and for the women of this country. It is a moment for which we have waited over two hundred years. Never losing faith, we waited through the many years of struggle to achieve our rights.

"But women weren't just waiting; they were working. Never losing faith, we worked to redeem the promise of America, that all men and women are created equal. For our daughters and granddaughters, today we have broken the marble ceiling. . . .

"We have made history, now let us make progress."

2

Declarations of Independence

I'll never forget the first time I saw the Capitol. It was on a cold January day in 1947, when I was six years old. The occasion was my father's swearing-in ceremony for his fifth term in Congress.

My brothers were excited. As our car approached the Capitol, they kept saying, "Nancy, look at the Capitol." I said I didn't see any capitals. They insisted, and finally I asked, "Is it a capital *A*, *B*, or *C*?" As we drove closer, my brother Joey turned my head toward the most amazing sight.

I didn't see the giant letters I expected. Instead, I saw a stunning building with a magnificent white dome. I still think it's the most beautiful building in the world because of what it represents: the voice of the people.

Whether to view it as the world's greatest symbol of democracy, to serve in it as a Representative of the people, or to preside over it as the Speaker of the House, any association with the Capitol is exciting.

To this day, I feel a strong connection to my father whenever I'm on the floor of the House, imagining what it must have been like for him to be one of the earliest Italian Americans to serve there. My father, Thomas D'Alesandro Jr., was a U.S. Congressman from Maryland, first elected in 1938 as a New Deal Democrat loyal to FDR. He later served as the Mayor of Baltimore for twelve years. My mother, Nancy (Annunciata in Italian) Lombardi, so named because she was born on March 25, the Feast of the Annunciation, was my father's teammate every step of the way.

Both of my parents were raised in Baltimore's Little Italy, as was I. My father's mother was born in Baltimore—his grandparents were from Venice and Genoa. His father was from Abruzzi.

My mother's father was born in Campobasso and her mother in Sicily. They met in Pawtucket, Rhode Island, and raised their family in Baltimore.

It was into this large Italian American family that I was born, the only daughter after six sons. We were devoutly

Catholic, deeply patriotic, proud of our Italian American heritage, and staunchly Democratic.

Those views were shared by our neighbors. Diversity in Little Italy was based on what part of Italy your family was from. Every region and food of Italy was represented in our neighborhood—Genovese, Napolitano, Abruzzese, Veneziano, Romano, Piemontese, Toscano, Siciliano, and more.

Growing up in Little Italy impressed upon me the vitality immigrants bring to America. With their courage, optimism, and determination to make the future better for their families, they fulfill the American dream. They made America stronger. That has been true throughout American history, and it is true today.

My father was twenty-five and already a member of the Maryland State Legislature when he noticed a beautiful nineteen-year-old woman leaving St. Leo's Church one Sunday morning. He followed her down the street and, when she stopped at a corner, went up to her and asked for a date.

My mother's response was to tell the dapper legislator that she didn't know who he was and that she would not go out on a date unless her grandmother approved. Hence Daddy's courtship of Mommy's grandmother.

Apparently he passed inspection because my mother

and he were married in a wedding that was a traffic-stopping event in Baltimore. All of the members of the Baltimore Police and Fire Departments were invited.

Daddy's introduction to government began at the age of eight, when his mother took him to the 1912 Democratic Convention, not far from their home in Little Italy. I can imagine Daddy's thrill at hearing the roars coming from inside the Fifth Regiment Armory, where William Jennings Bryan nominated the soon-to-be President Woodrow Wilson, who won the nomination on the forty-sixth ballot.

When he was old enough to vote, my father cast his first vote ever for himself in a successful election to the Maryland House of Delegates. He went from there to the Baltimore City Council and then on to Congress before serving as Mayor.

My father was a phenomenal natural politician, handsome, and charismatic. With his piercing blue eyes, pencil-thin moustache, and trademark polka-dot bow ties, he cut a dashing figure. He was a talented dancer and a brilliant orator. Although he did not have much formal education, he was clever and determined. He was very knowledgeable in a number of areas, especially public policy.

Except for his earliest years in politics, my mother was his partner. She was smart, and she had a sense of justice that became a driving force in our family's life. I often think she was born fifty years too soon. The truth is that my father and the times held her back.

Now, my father was a wonderful man with an enormous heart, very charming and smart, very loyal, a public servant in the truest sense. While he was forward-thinking and progressive, and appreciated the growing role women were playing in politics, he was bound by the old traditions when it came to his own family. My father did not even want me to cut my long hair when I was a young teenager.

My mother was a wonderful wife and parent, and she was also an entrepreneur and a visionary. She started law school but had to stop when three of her sons had whooping cough at the same time. She made astute investments, but Daddy would not sign off on them (which, sadly, would have been necessary at the time). She had a patent on the first device to apply steam to the face, which she called Velvex—Beauty by Vapor. It was her brainchild, and she had customers throughout the United States, but Daddy wanted her close to home.

Despite her frequent clashes of will with Daddy, she loved her marriage, though I think it's fair to say she didn't recommend marrying young. Whenever she heard that a young woman was getting married, she'd say, "I don't know why she's rushing into this. She has all this talent, all this spirit and intelligence—why does anyone have to get married so young?"

Of course, she was thinking back over her own life. She had dreams of her own, and part of what makes me so receptive to new possibilities, I suspect, is knowing that she could not pursue hers.

I learned to assert my independence early. I'm not saying I was particularly rebellious, but with all of those older brothers, I did have to find ways to hold my own.

One of our family stories involves my brother Joey and me at our father's first inauguration as Mayor of Baltimore. We all went to City Hall, and my parents and the three older boys were busy greeting guests. My brothers Hector and Joey and I were ushered into a side room to draw and color until the ceremony began.

We, like all families, had a steadfast rule that the children were never allowed to speak to strangers. When a tall, distinguished gentleman came into the room and said, "Hello, how are you?" I would not utter a word in reply.

"Your father is going to be the Mayor. Isn't that exciting?" he said.

Still not a word from me, but my brothers were saying, "It's all right, we can say hello." It turned out that the gentleman was Theodore Roosevelt McKeldin, the outgoing Mayor of Baltimore, and we were in his private office.

Joey said to me that he was going to tell Mommy that I was not polite to the Mayor.

"If you do," I said calmly, "I will tell Mommy that you talked to a stranger."

I had just turned seven, and Joey was nine. I didn't squeal on him, and because I'd earned his respect, he didn't squeal on me.

I had just built my first strategic alliance.

In the summer our family went to Ocean City, Maryland, which was heaven on earth. In those days it was a sleepy village with a boardwalk about twenty-five blocks long. At one end were the arcades and tourist attractions and at the other were the homes and hotels.

In the middle was Ninth Street—the center of our social life—where teenagers and college students converged in the evening. When I was old enough, my girlfriends and I would go there to meet up with friends. Two of my best friends were Sally McGeehan and Nancy Hepburn. We would make the Ninth Street scene and go home for the early curfew set by my parents, while others went to beach parties.

For weeks our family (with Daddy joining us on the weekends) enjoyed the beach, the salt air, and Maryland steamed crabs and fresh corn on the cob. Our rented home was a gathering place where friends from Baltimore and around the state would stop by and spend time chatting on the porch. The rocking chairs, the passing parade of vacationers, and the unimpeded view of the Atlantic Ocean were all very relaxing.

I loved our time "down the ocean," as they say in Maryland. Later, when I was dating Paul Pelosi, a Californian, I used to tell him that his biggest competition was the Atlantic Ocean, which I never wanted to leave.

At the shore, my protective family found many opportunities to impede my independence. My parents came up with strict rules for me—in addition to the too-early (in my opinion) curfew, they also decreed that there would be no bike riding in the street (only on the boardwalk) and no waterskiing (far too dangerous).

I, of course, rode my bicycle on the street anyway.

I also learned to water-ski, and they got used to it—after a while.

But they saved their most humiliating restrictions for the Atlantic Ocean. My friends and I would take surf mats down the beach and go out as far as we dared.

That was fine, except that sometimes the tide would

take us right in front of our rental house, where my parents (and sometimes my brothers, too) would spot us and start waving their arms and demanding that we be whistled in by the beach patrol. It was embarrassing, but the next day we would start all over again.

As for going out far beyond the waves, seeing the movie *Jaws* years later would keep my children and me close to shore.

My mother, despite her own thwarted ambitions, had to struggle against her instinct to hold me close. She always said she wanted me to have roots and wings. Roots—a sense of belonging. Wings—the freedom to fly away and experience life on my own terms.

But she sometimes had trouble with the wings part.

She wanted to protect me from the world, with all its potential heartaches and disappointments. And in her mind, the answer to this dilemma was simple: I should become a nun.

As I entered my teen years I knew that was not going to happen. I was a typical 1950s teenager who wore blouses with Peter Pan collars and circle pins. My girlfriends and I loved cinch belts, crinolines, charm bracelets, and matching sweater sets. We wore our hair in ponytails or pixie cuts and danced to the music of Elvis Presley.

In time, Mommy got used to the idea that I was not

going to become a nun. I adored my mother, and loved her with all my heart, but I let her know, gently, that my life was my own.

Years later, when I was a mother myself, I faced similar situations about letting go of my own five children. I remember advice someone gave me that I never forgot: Hold on to your children too tightly, and they will be like mercury. As soon as you open your hand, mercury scatters.

You want them to grow up to be happy, fulfilled, independent adults. At the same time, you worry about them.

I remember asking Daddy, "When do you stop worrying about your children?" And he said, "Not until they go onto Social Security."

As any mother will attest, the instinct to look after our children stays with us long after they need our attention. Even when my children were older, for years, at quarter to noon, I would get this sudden feeling in the pit of my stomach that said, "I've got to go pick up my car pool." A quarter to twelve was the pickup time for preschool.

When they began elementary school, the feeling migrated to 3:00 P.M. *I have to get my car pool,* I would think. Then, one by one, they wanted to go by bus with their friends. But the feeling in my stomach continued for a long time.

Their preference for taking the bus had its exceptions.

One morning when it was pouring rain, the children came into our room to ask for a ride to school. Paul, who of course would drive them there, turned and joked, "No, go out into the rain and shrink. We want our babies back."

Among our children, Paul Jr. was determined to carve out his own path early on, and I could certainly relate to his situation. He was the only boy, with four sisters; I had been the only daughter, with five brothers.

When he was old enough to begin kindergarten, Paul balked at the idea of going to the same school as his sisters, the Convent of the Sacred Heart. He made his views known during his defiant interview at the school when he was five.

On his first day at the school of his choice, Town School for Boys, he came home with his name tag tied with yarn around his wrist. His sister Jacqueline very protectively told him that he was supposed to wear it around his neck.

"At my school, my teacher said I can wear it anywhere I want," Paul Jr. replied. "You don't go to my school, you weren't there, so you couldn't possibly know." This was a historic day in our house. It was Paul Jr.'s declaration of independence from the tyranny of a household of girls.

Of course, having been in his shoes, I understood.

But years later, apparently I forgot.

When I was elected to Congress, Christine, Jacqueline, and Paul Jr. were attending Georgetown University. I had the brilliant idea that they could all move in with me, thereby saving their rents and upgrading their living quarters.

Christine lived with her friends in a basement apartment, Jacqueline in an attic with seven friends and one bathroom, and Paul Jr. in a freshman dorm. Though it wasn't readily apparent to me, these places were heaven on earth to the kids.

There was a swift response: "Mother, not only do we not want to live with you, we don't want to live with each other. We love our siblings, but we want to live with our friends. We are in college, you are in Congress. Why don't you just forget we are in the same city?"

In my defense I noted that I would only be in Washington three nights a week. To which they said, "How would you have liked it if your mother came to live with you when you were in college?"

What could I have been thinking? They were, of course, right. And so I got the message that they wanted their space. Still, their presence in Washington made my coming to Congress much easier. Just the thought that I might see the children helped me get on the plane to leave our home in San Francisco each week.

3

An Open House

From a very early age, my brothers and I were taught to be compassionate and to be aware of the world around us. Helping others was part of daily life in the D'Alesandro household. People knew that this was where Congressman D'Alesandro lived, and would line up at our door, looking for help. It was the same when my father became Mayor. Some people needed work. Others needed a bed in City Hospital or housing in the projects. Sometimes they were just looking for something to eat.

They would file in, past the very large portraits of Presidents Roosevelt and Truman in the front room, and sit at my mother's desk. Some were immigrants who spoke no English, and she conversed with them in Italian. Our home was truly an "open house."

During the Great Depression, before I was born, my brother Tommy recalls that it was common for people who were seeking help to join the family at the dinner table. My mother would just add a few more ingredients to the stew and invite them in.

She was an incredible asset to my father, and to the people of Baltimore. She, too, was a public servant. She was not paid, and she held no elected or appointed position, but she considered it part of her duty to contribute what she could. I think she knew everyone in the Housing Authority, the hospitals, and the courts in the City of Baltimore.

Part of the system of the home office was something we called the "favor file." When someone came in with a request, Mommy wrote it down on a piece of yellow paper and put it in a folder. Then, when that person got on his or her feet and someone else came in looking for similar help, my mother would take out the slip of paper and call on the first person to help the second. In this way, the responsibility of doing good was passed forward.

And the rest of us had to pitch in. Even when I was a little girl, I, too, could tell someone whom to call to get on welfare, get into City Hospital, or be accepted in the projects. I wasn't allowed to open the door to strangers, of course, but I did answer the phone, and I knew exactly what Mommy would tell them. I heard her say it so many times.

This felt totally natural to my brothers and me. It was part of our father's duty as a public servant; it was part of our sense of community in Little Italy; and it was part of our Catholic faith.

Even though I was often exposed to people in need, I vividly remember going to a friend's house where they didn't have enough to eat, and it had a profound effect on me. It was unusual for me to be allowed to go to someone else's home unless my parents were friends with their parents. But one little girl, whose family was not known to us, had come to our house a number of times, and her mother had invited me for dinner. My brothers walked me there and waited outside until I was ready to go home. When we were finished eating, my friend's mother took the half-eaten food off of all our plates—not leftovers, but half-eaten food—and scraped it back into a bowl for the next day.

I couldn't believe my eyes. I thought, *Oh, my God, if I'd only known, I would have saved a few more things on my plate.* There they were, proudly sharing a meal with me, even though this was all they would have to eat tomorrow.

I knew many people who were poor, but it was entirely different to see this at their table.

We are devout Catholics, and service to others is a fundamental part of our faith. From first grade through high school I attended the Institute of Notre Dame in Baltimore, where my mother had also gone. The School Sisters of Notre Dame were ambitious for our futures, and part of their expectations for us was that we would never forget the needy, the sick, and the vulnerable. Barbara Mikulski, who would become the first woman elected to the Senate in her own right, is also a graduate of I.N.D.

The curriculum was rigorous and decorum was emphasized. In the vestibule of the school was a framed statement that said, "School is not a Prison, it is not a Playground, it is Time, it is Opportunity." Our Catholic education was shaped by the Baltimore Catechism, and our personal holiness was guided by the nuns in addition to our parents.

It was the nuns, in fact, who wrote my first public "speech," which was exactly one sentence long, and which I recited at my father's swearing-in ceremony as Mayor when I was seven years old. I was brought to the podium, which was ringed with microphones. With newspaper photographers' flashbulbs popping, wearing my new blue suit and white hat, I held the Bible to swear in my father.

After he took the oath I presented him with the Bible

with these words: "Dear Daddy, I hope this holy book will guide you to be a good man."

Daddy, of course, was already a good man. Both my parents were driven by a sense of justice and fairness. Years later, at my mother's funeral Mass, Baltimore's Cardinal Keeler referred to her as "Annunciata Regina"— Queen Nancy—for her good works and the respect she enjoyed in the community. My brothers and I used to say that our parents were working on the side of the angels, and now they are with them.

My upbringing taught me the significance of religious faith and how people rely on it to get through life's travails and hardships. This realization has served me well in life and in politics.

I saw, with my own mother, the importance of faith in surviving personal tragedy. My parents actually had six sons, not five. One of them, Nicholas, died of pneumonia at age three. (They later had another son who was also named Nicholas.) It happened before I was born, but my brother Tommy remembers our mother weeping inconsolably. She always told me that not a single day went by, for the rest of her life, that she didn't think of little Nicky. Indeed, she prayed to him, and I saw how her strong faith got her through.

In the 1950s, our faith was not only personal but

extended to the world. At home, at school, and in church we prayed for the conversion of atheistic Russia. My mother had a special devotion to freeing Hungarian Cardinal Jozsef Mindszenty, imprisoned by the Soviets for his religious beliefs—and because the Soviets were threatened by his large following. He wrote a book from prison that included thoughts about his mother. Based on his writings, Mommy wrote a poem-prayer dedicated to her mother, whom she worshipped, which begins:

"Mother, I think of you, Guardian Angel of my childhood. Who can fathom the real meaning of the word mother? Whose hearts are not filled with the memory of her, who has never stopped loving us from the first moment of our existence, when, like a ray of sunshine she beamed down into our cradles! Even when the word is spoken by an old man it sounds as if it comes from the lips of a child."

Growing up Catholic had an enormous impact on me—greater, I am certain, than growing up in a political family. I knew it then, and I know it now. That realization would come home to me again on the day I was nominated by the House Democrats to be Speaker.

Our caucus chair, Rahm Emanuel, whispered his congratulations. His kind words startled me and brought me right back to Albemarle Street in Baltimore. When I took the microphone, I told my colleagues that Rahm had said my parents would be so proud. But I told them that my parents didn't raise me to be Speaker, *they raised me to be holy.* That was their measure of a successful child.

Many of my friends were drawn to politics by the calling of their faith and the words of the Bible. For many in my generation, our greatest political inspiration was John F. Kennedy. It's clear that his sense of responsibility to all people was a combination of his patriotic upbringing and the teachings of the Church. Many of the nuns at the Institute of Notre Dame were Irish and from Boston, and they often spoke of the Kennedys—their faith, patriotism, and pride of family.

I had a chance to meet John Kennedy in 1957, when he was the guest speaker at a dinner sponsored by the United Nations Association of Maryland. He was already a political celebrity as a Senator from Massachusetts, and a contender to be Adlai Stevenson's running mate in the 1956 election. The nuns at my school considered Kennedy's visit a historic occasion, and I wanted to attend his speech.

Knowing of my excitement, my mother said she wasn't feeling well, and let me go in her place. And her place, as the First Lady of Baltimore, was at the head table, seated next to Senator Kennedy.

One of the other tables at the dinner was reserved for students who were members of the United Nations Association. We had a chapter at the Institute of Notre Dame and I was a member. At one point, I was invited by the high school group to join their table.

I had no difficulty saying, "Thank you so much, I wish I could, but I am representing my mother, so I have to stay here." My encounter with history trumped my usual courtesy, but I knew the nuns would approve. Senator Kennedy was amused, and the high schoolers were happy to have found an excuse to come to the head table and be introduced to the Senator, who made us all feel very important by asking about our studies in high school.

In the course of the evening a photographer took my picture with Senator Kennedy. A formally dressed woman said to me, "Save this picture—one day he may be President." Little did we know that the photo would be proudly displayed half a century later in the office of the Speaker of the House.

A few years after this occasion came the time we were waiting for—the Presidential election of 1960 and the candidacy of John F. Kennedy. Daddy was the Democratic National Committeeman from Maryland and an early Kennedy supporter. Because my father had a fear of flying we took the train from Baltimore to the Democratic National Convention in Los Angeles.

On the way, we stopped in San Francisco, the first time I visited the exciting city that would one day be my home. We all loved it, and, looking back, I believe that visit probably made it easier for my parents to accept my later moving so far from them.

At the convention in Los Angeles, we had front-row seats and special access to the Kennedy events. The enthusiasm of the Democrats was so great that Senator Kennedy's acceptance speech had to be moved to the L.A. Coliseum. To witness the first Catholic being nominated was a proud moment for those of us who shared Kennedy's religion at a time when there was still great discrimination when it came to the Presidency. We all worked hard for his election and looked forward to his Inauguration.

Because Daddy was a former Member of Congress, we had great seats on the Capitol steps and a clear view of the future on that freezing cold day in January 1961 when JFK challenged us all with his famous speech:

"My fellow Americans, ask not what your country can do for you—ask what you can do for your country."

Everyone knows that line. But as a Congresswoman involved in foreign affairs, I often quote the words that follow it:

"My fellow citizens of the world: ask not what America will do for you, but what together we can do for the freedom of man."

Everyone said that the youth, vigor, and vitality of the Kennedy presidency brought Washington to life. He made my generation believe that anything was possible. Many of us were attracted to public service. We wanted to reach out, to make a difference in our country and in the world.

My father proudly served in the Kennedy Administration, and I would study the Kennedy Presidency in college.

My public service would come later.

4

Love Happens

When it was time for me to apply to college, I set my sights on Trinity College in Washington, D.C., the oldest women's Catholic college in America. I thought my parents were more likely to let me go away if I went to a Catholic, all-women's school only a short distance from Baltimore.

When I was accepted, my mother and I were thrilled. But this time it was my father's turn to be protective. Daddy had hoped I would go to college in Baltimore and live at home. Poor Daddy! With Mommy as my ally, he didn't stand a chance.

Driving from the streets of Washington onto the Trinity campus, with its serenely beautiful gardens and lawns, was like entering Shangri-La. Arriving on the first day, in the fall of 1958, I knew immediately that I would be happy there. Growing up in politics was exciting, but I welcomed the relative normalcy of college. After living with five older brothers, I was overjoyed at the prospect of living with girlfriends.

On the very first day, I met classmates who became my friends for life. Rita Murray (from Riverdale, New York), Celia Lynett (from Scranton, Pennsylvania), and I were assigned to the same hall. We sometimes say we bonded immediately because we all had so many brothers—Rita had five and Celia had three. Mary Catherine McGarraghy, who was from Washington and lived at home with her parents, also became part of our group.

We met at the welcoming reception. Some of the students knew one another from back home. I didn't know a soul. One of the first students I met was Martha Dodd. While I was enjoying being away from the political world for the first time in my life, Martha came over to me, looked at my name tag, and said, "Nancy D'Alesandro—is your father running for Senate?"

"How did you know?" I whispered.

Martha said she had seen Daddy's campaign billboards in Maryland when her parents were driving her to Trinity.

She noticed because her father, Thomas Dodd, was also running for Senate.

We agreed that we wouldn't talk about it to our classmates.

Thus began my new, normal existence. As delighted as I was to be at Trinity, my feelings were complicated. I loved Trinity, but I secretly cried for two weeks because I missed my family.

Sometimes I wished that my mother could have had the same freedom when she was young. Mommy would have loved Trinity. It was intellectually demanding, and the Sisters of Notre Dame de Namur, who taught us, knew most of us would marry and have families. At the same time, they wanted us to develop our minds to think about the world beyond us and to continue studies past college.

I had intended to major in political science, but at Trinity at that time you had to major in history in order to study political science. Our teachers often quoted the great English historian J. R. Seeley's aphorism:

History without political science has no fruit,
Political science without history has no root.

The combination was perfect. In studying about America's Founding Fathers, we learned about the qualities of leadership that were essential to establishing our country. Those same qualities were important in keeping our union together and are necessary for taking us into the future. We learned that leadership requires vision, judgment, action, and the respect of the American people. No matter how excellent the intellectual appeal, the emotional connection is essential for success.

A President's vision and judgment enable him or her to act intuitively to make the right decision. When we were studying these aspects of leadership, I couldn't help think about how women were especially blessed with heightened intuition to decide or to advise.

I began to think my future might include law school. I had no interest in settling down and getting married at a young age.

But I hadn't counted on meeting Paul Pelosi.

Young women sometimes ask me what is the "right way" or the "best path" to take in life—to get married and have children, to put that off until later, to pursue a career, or to do both at the same time. My answer, based on my experience, is that there is no "right" or "best" path—there is only your path. While much depends on our choices, there is also an element of chance—some call it fate—in which our path is altered when a special person comes along.

I was from Baltimore, Paul was from San Francisco, and I like to say we met in Africa, south of the Sahara. Actually, it wasn't the continent; it was a summer course on the subject at Georgetown University.

Although I had met Paul casually before, my first recollection of him during the first week of summer school was at Teehan's, a gathering spot for students near Georgetown University's School of Foreign Service. One of my friends asked Paul where his classes were being held, and when he responded, my friend said, "Oh, you're right next door to Nancy."

To which Paul replied, "Nancy who?"

Paul says he's been paying for that remark for a very long time.

A short time later, a group of us had gathered at the home of a Georgetown law student, Denny Meyer, who was engaged to my roommate, Rita Murray. It was a pleasant summer day and we were sitting in the living room with the windows open. We were talking about the Korean War, which some of us were studying at the time, and suddenly there was Paul, standing at the window.

"What are you guys talking about?" he asked.

"We're arguing about whether we should have crossed the Yalu River and gone into China," someone said.

Paul joined the conversation just as I was leaving to pick up my clothes before the cleaners closed. Paul pulled out a laundry ticket and said, "While you're there, will you pick up my shirts?" I took his ticket, put it in my pocket—and didn't give it another thought.

When I returned, Paul said, "I thought I had more shirts than that."

"I forgot all about your shirts," I said. My friends thought my response was amusing, and Paul found it intriguing. I really had forgotten about his shirts. But how could he *ever* have thought I would pick them up? After we were married, he once asked me to iron a shirt.

That didn't happen either.

Paul began to sit in on my class. His newfound (and, I hope, sincere) interest in Dr. Carroll Quigley's riveting lectures on African culture and languages led us to become friends. One evening, Sargent Shriver, the first Director of the Peace Corps, came to speak at Georgetown, and Paul introduced him to the audience. On the way in, Paul said to me casually, "When this is over, would you like to go out for a beer?"

"A beer?" I said. "I don't think so."

He was unruffled. "How about dessert?" Well, Paul had just stumbled across the key to my heart—chocolate. We went out for dessert, and that was the beginning of our relationship, which was a long way from being a romance.

When senior year began we started to date more frequently, but not exclusively. One day after Mass in Dahlgren Chapel at Georgetown, we were walking across campus and came to the Jesuit cemetery. The sight of the gravestones crowded close together in that small graveyard must have put us in a contemplative mood, and we talked about Jesuit philosophy and about life.

"What are you going to do when you grow up?" I asked Paul in a joking way.

He surprised me with his response.

"I'm going to come looking for you," he said. That was my first clue that he thought we might have a future together. Or else it was a really good line.

A year later, Paul proposed in Dahlgren Chapel. To this day, I can still conjure up the total joy of that moment. Afterward, we drove up to Baltimore and Paul proudly asked for my hand in marriage. My father, like many dads, was not eager to give his daughter away to anyone, although by then he knew Paul and had come to like him very much.

But more than anything else, Daddy did not want to be the one to tell his wife. He told us we had to do it.

My mother was almost sad when we told her. "Oh, my," she said. "Oh, my."

She turned to me with tears in her eyes. "I thought you'd always be with us," she said.

I thought (but did not say), *You also thought I was going to be a nun.*

Instead, I smiled and said, "Mommy, I love Paul. I want to marry him."

The weekend before I got married, the March on Washington for Jobs and Freedom was held. I went to add my support and was struck by the dignity and solemnity of the occasion.

I couldn't stay long enough to hear the Reverend Dr. Martin Luther King Jr. speak because I had to go to Baltimore to get ready for my wedding. The Pelosi family was coming several days early from California.

Though I didn't personally hear Dr. King's "I Have a Dream" speech, I was deeply moved reading about his "fierce urgency of now" exhortation the next day.

Today I have the honor of serving in Congress with another civil rights hero, Congressman John Lewis, who spoke at the March. Every day we are blessed by his calls to action and his wise advice to keep our eyes on the prize.

————————

At our beautiful wedding on September 7, 1963, my mother was radiant—she saw how happy I was—and Daddy dazzled my friends with his ballroom dancing until the rock-and-roll band started. Immediately after our honeymoon, Paul and I settled in New York City. I was twenty-three years old and newly married, and my world revolved around my husband.

New York was the only place Paul and I ever lived outside the orbit of either of our families. We had New York. We had each other. And, in what seemed like no time at all, we had three little girls: Nancy Corinne, Christine, born eighteen months later, and Jacqueline, born one year after Christine.

In addition to our little family in New York, we had Vince Wolfington. Paul and Vince met in their senior year at Malvern Prep, outside of Philadelphia, and went on to become roommates at Georgetown and in New York before we were married. They both worked for banks, Vince at Chase Manhattan and Paul at First National City Bank. After a few years Vince met his future wife, Alicia Usera, and they have been part of the Trinity/Georgetown group to this day.

I was a very happy young wife and mother, and for the time being I put aside my thoughts of law school. My life revolved around diapers, feeding schedules, playtime in the park, errands with babies in tow—and I loved it.

The only time I had to myself was when my babies went down for their nap. The second they were in bed, and before I started on the laundry, I would sit down to my *New York Times* crossword puzzle and a dish of chocolate ice cream. That was my survival strategy: my crossword puzzles and my chocolate.

It still is today.

I was in my own little world, though I still kept up with current affairs. I even volunteered during the 1966 midterm elections, although I certainly don't claim to have done very much—just some leafleting in our neighborhood for Democratic candidates (while pushing my babies in a stroller).

I followed politics with great interest and felt personally connected through my brother Tommy, who had followed in our father's footsteps and became Mayor of Baltimore in 1967. Tommy was a brilliant politician in his own right, and a forceful speaker, though in a very different way from our father.

Tommy was cooler, more modern, and more measured than Daddy—and he needed every ounce of his equanimity for his term in office, which coincided with the racial disturbances that occurred in Baltimore and other urban centers across America. He had to stand up for a principle in which he believed deeply—racial equality—in a city that had held on tightly to many of its old ways of thinking. This made him an extremely unpopular figure in some quarters. He jokes now (it's much easier to joke now) that when he used to ride in parades, the booing on some blocks would start even before he appeared.

Tommy was on the front lines; I was raising my babies. But the strange and terrible events of 1968 drew all Americans into the political debate.

The war in Vietnam was raging. In March, President Johnson announced he wouldn't run for reelection; just days later, Martin Luther King Jr. was assassinated. With the upcoming Democratic Convention, the party was bitterly split into factions.

My brother Tommy was for Bobby Kennedy; my father, now the senior statesman, was for Hubert Humphrey. Daddy and Tommy fought against each other at the Maryland State Convention to win delegates for their candidates, and it was a serious, generational fight.

Then Bobby Kennedy was assassinated, and Tommy was devastated.

Bobby Kennedy's death and that of Dr. King brought back horrible memories from five years earlier, when John Kennedy was killed in Dallas and America was plunged into sadness and disbelief.

We went to the very divided Democratic National Convention in Chicago—Tommy and his wife, Margie; Paul and I; and Daddy. Paul and I had a foot in both worlds: We were able to go onto the convention floor, and also get into the park across from our hotel to see the confrontations between the antiwar protestors and the baton-wielding police.

The convention itself was hardly less tumultuous, as security people hassled delegates and reporters. The rhetoric from the podium was heated. Mayor Richard Daley of Chicago was furious when Senator Abraham Ribicoff denounced the "Gestapo tactics" of the Chicago police.

Hubert Humphrey won the nomination, but the Democratic Party was still divided, particularly because Vice President Humphrey did not disassociate himself from Johnson's Vietnam War policy. I, too, opposed the war, but, wanting to get a Democrat in the White House, I stuffed many "Humphrey for President" leaflets under apartment doors that fall, visibly pregnant with my fourth child, and with my little girls in a stroller.

Someone once asked me if I was restless during that time, and I said no, because that implies some level of discontent. And I was personally content because for me, there was nothing more exciting than having and caring for new babies.

Yet I always knew that I did not want to deal only with the meals, the laundry, and the house forever. I still thought that I'd go to law school when the children were grown.

Although I never made it to law school, it is a source of satisfaction to me that the legislation we pass in Congress is being taught in law schools across America.

5

Be Open to the New

When Paul and I were married, I knew there was a good possibility I might be living in California someday. Paul loved his hometown, San Francisco.

Happily for me, San Francisco is a very Democratic city, and a very Italian American city as well. I had loved it ever since the first time I went there with my parents on the way to the 1960 Democratic National Convention in Los Angeles.

The decision for us to return to Paul's hometown was a sudden one. On the very day our fourth child, Paul Jr., was born in New York, January 23, 1969, Paul was offered an exciting job with a new publicly held financial services company located in San Francisco. It was a ground-floor opportunity in a brand-new market, at the dawn of the Silicon Valley tech boom. Paul said, "If we're ever going to go to California, now is the time."

Paul was the youngest of three sons in a family that had deep roots there. His parents, John and Corinne Bianchi Pelosi, were part of San Francisco's proud Italian American community. Both had been born in Italy in the early 1900s, John in the southern province of Potenza, Corinne in Tuscany, not far from Lucca. Both had immigrated to California, he as a young man, she as a small child with her parents.

They were both very special and kind people. John Pelosi was extremely well read and spoke five languages. Corinne ("Nana" to our family) was an angel—the ultimate mother and grandmother. They both loved their family, the opera, and their garden. Since the 1930s, they were devout parishioners of St. Vincent de Paul Catholic Church, which Paul and I still attend to this day.

Faith has always been important to the Pelosi family and would be a source of strength to them when they lost a son, "dear David" as Nana called him, who died in an automobile accident in 1957, and much later two granddaughters who died in a tragic fire.

Returning to San Francisco, we would be close to Paul's newly widowed mother and the family of his brother Ronald, who had become active in Democratic politics. In 1967, Ronald was elected to the San Francisco Board of Supervisors, and was later its president.

Paul Jr. was just four weeks old when we made the big move. As we trooped through the airport, I was confident that we were handling things pretty well with our baby boy and our three little daughters. Nancy Corinne was four, Christine was two and a half, and Jacqueline was eighteen months.

On the plane, after we had sung "California Here We Come" to the children for the third time, Paul turned to me and said, "There's just one thing I have to tell you. My mother would be *so sad* if, on our very first night in San Francisco, we didn't stay in her home."

I looked at my husband. He knew I'd thought we were staying at a hotel. It was supposed to be an adventure for the children. He also knew that I am a person who needs my own space.

We had made an agreement on two points that were important to me. One was that I would continue to get my *New York Times* every day after we moved to San Francisco. The second was that I wouldn't have to stay in anyone's home.

My mother-in-law, Nana, was a lovely person, and I never wanted to disappoint her. But I was not happy with this change in plans.

"Come on, Nancy," Paul said. "We'll just go there for one night, and then we'll move on."

We would be there for four months.

When we began looking for an apartment or house, no one, it seemed, wanted to rent to a large family. And so the search continued. Despite Nana's endless kindness, can you imagine living in your mother-in-law's house for four months with four small children? They were adorable but very active and disruptive because we didn't have our own space and routine. I tried to make the best of the situation.

One Sunday morning, Paul and I were in Nana's breakfast room together with the four children. Nana was in the next room. The little girls were playing on the floor as I fed the baby. Paul and I looked at each other, sized up the situation, and laughed.

I said, "At least we're happy; just think of what you'd be without us."

From the next room, to our complete surprise, without missing a beat, Nana's voice rang out loud and clear:

"An attorney!"

Paul and I burst into laughter. He knew that I was the one who had wanted to go to law school; he had lost interest in being an attorney years before. He hadn't even taken the LSAT, which I had.

Apparently, though, this had been Nana's dream for him all along—a dream that, from her perspective, had been thwarted by his early marriage and all those children.

Finally, after a few months of looking, the perfect rental appeared. It was a big home, already set up for a large family. It was childproofed and had a beautiful backyard with a swing set and sandbox.

I was thrilled. Ecstatic.

I was looking forward to living there, being independent and in control of my routine. Just before we sealed the deal, I asked why the house had become available.

"Oh," the owner said. "My husband has been appointed Deputy Secretary of the Department of Health, Education, and Welfare, so we'll be going back East to join the Nixon Administration."

My heart sank. "I'm sorry," I told the real estate agent, "but we won't be able to live here."

The real estate agent stared at me. "What?" she said after a second. She knew how many places we had looked at, only to be told by the owners—sometimes politely and sometimes not—that they'd rather rent to people with four dogs than four young children. She also knew how much I wanted to move out of my mother-in-law's home.

"We won't be able to live here," I repeated. "I could never live anyplace that was made available because of the election of Richard Nixon."

So, back to Nana's.

Our daughter, Alexandra, who hadn't been born yet, often says to me that she knows everything she needs to know about me by hearing that story.

Raising children is hard work. Two gifts for which I am grateful to my parents are a high level of energy and a strong work ethic. From my experience in a very tough political arena, where so much is at stake and the hours are endless, I can honestly say that the hardest job of all is raising a family. It gives you the most joy and it is wonderful to look back on, but doing it can be overwhelming. It is so constant. Mothers know this. Shortly after Nancy Corinne was born, my mother said to me, "Did you ever think that such a precious little bundle could be so much work?"

One day, when I was pushing Nancy Corinne and Christine in a stroller in New York and very pregnant with Jacqueline, a neighbor and mother of twin boys approached me and said, "Get help! Get help right now! If you can't afford it, borrow money from a bank, but get help!"

I didn't take her advice, but when we had more children it was almost impossible to get help because no one wanted to work for a family with five little children born in six years.

The work ethic and, frankly, the discipline that taking care of small children forces on you make any other job possible. I used to say that I had the best life and some of the worst days of anyone I knew. Some days I didn't even have time to wash my face. Just when you see the light at the end of the tunnel of years of diapers, you find out that the light is another train called homework, years of homework.

For the children's sake, and for your sanity, you can never let on to them that this is a struggle. But mothers know.

Paul and I started thinking that maybe we should buy, not rent, a house, and before long we found a great place. It was larger than we needed, and it required work, but it was on a beautiful, circular cul-de-sac called Presidio

Terrace, adjacent to the military base, a 1,491-acre preserve in the midst of the city.

There were many children in the neighborhood, and as our kids grew older, they each made their own circle of friends. It was a great place for playing outside, and there always seemed to be activity in the street—bike riding, kickball, skateboarding, hide-and-seek.

By the time we had four children in school and one in preschool, we had created our own routine. My children still tease me about our motto, "Proper preparation prevents poor performance."

In the morning, after they made their beds (required) and put their rooms in order (strongly suggested), they came down to the kitchen, where I would have breakfast waiting for them. Before we headed out the door, I would do an inspection of shoes, uniforms, and teeth. Paul and I would comb their hair. The big question was braids or ponytails, and one day, in our haste, Jacqueline went to school with one of each. Often as not, I was driving a car pool (occasionally with my nightgown on under my coat).

After school, they had a snack and started their homework, then went outside to play. My cardinal rule for moms (or just another survival tactic): Get the children out of the house. We had a big old brass cowbell, and when it was time for the children to come in for dinner, I would stand on the steps and ring it. It always amazed me how they came scurrying from various directions, even down from a tree.

After dinner the children and I began lunch bag preparations and set the table for breakfast, as is the routine in homes across America each evening. And then, more homework before lights out.

In addition to the children playing in Presidio Terrace, we spent a great deal of our time at Julius Kahn Playground in the Presidio. I met one of my first and lifelong San Francisco friends there, Kay Kimpton Walker, when our sons were playing in the sandbox. For a few summers our family went to Belvedere in Marin County, where we established a family friendship with Sally and Bill Hambrecht. The Walkers, the Hambrechts, and Kay and Frank Woods (even though the Woods are staunch Republicans) became our West Coast pals.

At that time our closest friends in the Terrace were strictly Democratic—Bob and Naomi Lauter, Barbara and Dick Sklar, and also the Guggenhimes (registration unknown). In San Francisco, we met most of our friends through our children, and our families have remained close. Because of an introduction by our good friends Gordon and Ann Getty, I served on the L. S. B. Leakey

Foundation for several years. I enjoyed learning much more about paleoanthropology, the origins of man, and the behavior of primates, and it was a great introduction to science for our children. When they were little they were thrilled to meet Jane Goodall, and when they were older they got to go on a dig with Richard Leakey in Kenya.

Our home would turn out to play an important role in my political future, so perhaps we were destined to live there. When we first moved in, a friend came by and said, "Oh, you have a large house, we'll be having lots of Democratic events here." We laughed. But it turned out to be true.

The house was indeed large enough to host political events, and at a time when there wasn't much else I could offer the Democratic Party, Paul and I were able, at least, to volunteer our hospitality. I found it funny that our guests would invariably say, "How smart of you to take out most of your furniture before the party so more people could fit!" And I'd think, *But this* is *the furniture.*

My occupation was full-time mom, so anything else I did was strictly on a volunteer basis and without an official position. Then one day I received a phone call from Joe Alioto, the Mayor of San Francisco.

The Mayor was our neighbor, three doors down. Paul had known and coached the older Alioto children when he was growing up. And there was another connection: Mayor Alioto and my brother Tommy had become mayors of major American cities at exactly the same time, and they knew each other well. Still, I was curious about this five o'clock phone call.

"So what are you doing, Nancy?" Joe Alioto asked. "Making a great big pot of *pasta e fagioli*?"

I smiled and shook my head. Joseph Alioto was a dynamic politician and a brilliant former classics scholar who often referred to ancient Greek and Roman history in his speeches. He also had a touch of old-school thinking, and assumed that the only thing I could be doing at five in the afternoon was cooking.

I responded, "No, I am not making *pasta e fagioli*. I'm reading the newspaper."

"That's nice, that's nice," he said. "Listen, Nancy. I'm just calling because I want to appoint you to the Library Commission. I think it's time for you to get official recognition of your work, and that's what I'm calling to tell you."

"Oh, Mr. Mayor," I said, "I don't need official recognition. I'm happy to work as a volunteer. I love the library and I love Kevin."

Kevin Starr had recently come back from Harvard with his wife, Sheila, and was now the City Librarian of San Francisco. Mayor Alioto's appointee, he was shaking things up at the library, and some of the board members were unhappy. I recognized instantly that the Mayor wanted to appoint one more friendly vote.

"Now, Kevin needs you, and I need you," he said. "And besides," he added, "what's all this about volunteering and getting no official recognition? One day you might want to run for office; it will help that you were recognized in the city as a commissioner. This is important."

"Mr. Mayor," I said, "I have absolutely no intention of running for office."

"Nancy, you love the library; this is perfect for you. Why don't you think about it?"

I thought of the many happy hours I'd spent as a girl at the Enoch Pratt Free Library in Baltimore with its beautiful children's library and, later, the H. L. Mencken Room. I thought about how much I loved words, books, libraries—and San Francisco.

I decided to accept the appointment.

When I was a commissioner, the Library Commission decided to give more people an opportunity to participate by moving its meetings out of the main library and into the community, to the smaller library branches throughout the city. I quickly learned that when I went to these meetings and showed up as a commissioner with a vote, people cared about what I thought. They called me to ask my opinions. I was now officially involved in the community. And I loved it.

Although my roots were in Baltimore, and that is where my journey began, moving to San Francisco put me on an interesting and challenging path. It was my brothers who stayed close to home. They grew up to be remarkable men, each in his own way. Four of them proudly served our country in the military. All five of them—Thomas III, Franklin Roosevelt, Nicholas, Hector, and Joseph—were each involved, at one time or another, in public service for the city of Baltimore.

I was the one, it seemed, who was destined to fly away.

PART TWO

KITCHEN TO CONGRESS

6

Recognize Opportunity

E ven though my political career was in California, as fate would have it, my springboard into a higher level of politics was a Maryland connection. It came when Jerry Brown decided to run for President in 1976.

Jerry was the newly elected Governor of California. He was both a progressive Democrat and a fiscal conservative, and he started making waves as soon as he took office with his strong stand on environmental issues and his "small is beautiful" philosophy. He lived in a small apartment instead of the Governor's mansion and rode in a compact car instead of a limousine. In a few national interviews, he had established himself as a celebrity and a voice of the future.

Although Jerry's family had been friends of the Pelosis, I didn't know him well. Paul knew him much better than I did. Jerry had been in the same class as Paul's brother David at St. Ignatius High School. There were also connections between the Brown and Ronald Pelosi families.

When Jerry decided to run for President, it was already March, which was very late in the game. The California primary was to be in June, and Jerry's campaign would focus on making its strongest stand there.

But the logic of this strategy worried me. I knew a great deal would happen before June. One day, when I was talking to my friend Leo McCarthy, who was Speaker of the California State Assembly and the chair of Jerry's Presidential campaign, I shared my concerns. "If Jerry Brown wants to run for President, we shouldn't wait for California," I told Leo. "By then it's going to be too late— there will already be a nominee. If he wants to win in California and control his own state party, he really has to run sooner."

I was very aware that Maryland's Presidential primary was in April, two months ahead of California's. And the Maryland Secretary of State had recently declared that a recognized candidate in any state in the union would automatically be on the ballot there.

So I said to Leo, "Let's go to Maryland. We can

begin the fight there." Leo talked to Jerry, and Jerry was interested.

My brother Tommy had finished his term as Mayor of Baltimore in 1971 and still had a high profile in the state. Tommy was intrigued by Jerry's ideas and national possibilities, and encouraged the Governor's campaign. Tommy enlisted a mutual friend of ours, Ted Venetoulis, who was the Baltimore County Executive and had a large grassroots organization, which immediately went to work.

Once Jerry signed off, we were on our way. Jerry came in on the first night of the campaign, and we had a huge rally at a hotel in downtown Baltimore. Thousands of people—most of them young—showed up to see him. The crowd was so large it spilled out into the street, and they cheered practically every word he said.

It was the same all over the state: People came by the thousands to see him.

After three short weeks of intense campaigning, Jerry won the popular vote in Maryland, and would go on to win more primaries. Even though the nomination would eventually go to Jimmy Carter, Jerry had established a real national presence.

A few days after the Maryland primary, when he came back to California, people were very excited. There was a huge welcoming party, and Jerry stood up and said, "Nancy Pelosi was the architect of my Maryland campaign."

In August I went to the Democratic National Convention in New York City as a delegate from California—and a new member of the Democratic National Committee. My political hobby had suddenly taken a serious turn. I think Mayor Alioto would have agreed that I now had at least one foot outside the kitchen.

I am frequently asked what event started me on my path from homemaker to House Speaker, and I cite the Brown campaign as being pivotal. And so does Jerry Brown. One can only see in retrospect the steps taken that got you from there to here. They will vary from person to person, but in all instances, steps were taken. By recognizing opportunities, assessing risks, and taking action, success can be achieved.

That fall, I received a call that Jerry wanted me to run for chair of the California Democratic Party.

I was honored, but I was also taken aback. The California Democratic Party is the largest state Democratic Party in the country. My political activities to date had chiefly involved helping Democratic candidates, which can be different from working inside the party. Moreover, the chairmanship was an elective office, although the Governor's endorsement could be tantamount to election.

From a political viewpoint, I thought Jerry's choice of me would not be well received. I had never been to a state party meeting; I had never been involved in the State Central Committee. I simply didn't have the experience. Moreover, two other leading Democrats, highly regarded in the party, were in the midst of a very hard-fought battle for the chairmanship. Both would be strong Jerry Brown supporters.

My response was, "Please find someone else."

At this point, Speaker Leo McCarthy said, "Jerry wants his own person in there. Why don't you run for Northern Chair of the party? Then nobody would have to be pushed aside for the top job."

Leo, as always, was right, and in 1977 I was elected Northern Chair of the California Democratic Party. The title of my campaign flyer was "Nancy Pelosi—Volunteer."

After serving two two-year terms, I went on to run for the state chairmanship, and won overwhelmingly. In both positions, I became knowledgeable about the entire state. People frequently talk about the differences between northern and southern California, but what I learned is that the real difference in California is between east and west.

Inland California voters tend to be moderate. On the coast, they tend to be progressive. As Party Chair, I had learned how to calibrate our issues so that I could try to unite all of the Democrats. That experience has served me well at the national level.

When I was Chair of the state party, we made a bid for the Democratic National Convention to be held in San Francisco in 1984. The competition was keen, and with the leadership of civic leader Walter Shorenstein, then-Mayor Dianne Feinstein, Speaker Willie Brown, and the Host Committee, which I chaired, we won.

Roz Wyman was Chair of the Convention Committee and we would become the best of friends. With her diplomacy and leadership, Roz planned an outstanding convention, accommodating the huge delegations of supporters for both Walter Mondale and Gary Hart. Everyone looked forward to Governor Mario Cuomo's keynote address. He was spectacular as he presented a vision of "the shining city on the hill."

When it was clear that Mondale would be the nominee, he announced that Geraldine Ferraro would be his running mate, the first woman in history to be on a major-party ticket.

It is hard to describe the depth of feeling that Geraldine's nomination sparked on the convention floor and beyond. The response she received was tumultuous and joyful. Although the Mondale-Ferraro ticket did not win in November, with her nomination, new ground had been broken for women.

7

Organize, Don't Agonize

After the election in November, I was encouraged by my friends in politics to run for Chair of the Democratic National Committee. Paul was asked what he thought, and I'll never forget what he said: "I want to help her all I can because this is the first thing she has wanted to do for herself."

It was a sweet thought, but I was surprised because I didn't see it that way. Paul's support, as it turned out, was especially important because almost immediately, several of my Democratic friends started an assault to tear me down. I understood that some of my friends would not be able to support me, and I respected their decision and their loyalty to others. I wouldn't say I was surprised, but

I was saddened by those who attacked me. As they say, the people closest to you politically are in a position to hurt you the most.

It was a disappointing loss, but I was strengthened by it. There was a saying among my political friends that would stand me in good stead: "Organize, don't agonize." Two years later, when Sala asked me to run for her Congressional seat, I was battle-ready.

Running for Sala's seat meant stepping into very big shoes. Sala was an impressive woman. She overlooked nothing, and when she took her husband's seat in Congress after his premature death, she proved to be an effective legislator. Having worked alongside Phillip for all those years, she knew the Congress inside and out. Her slogan was "Effective from the Start," and indeed she was.

Phillip Burton had first gone to the State Assembly in the mid-1950s; he was elected to Congress in 1964. Tall, physically powerful, and overbearing in his opinions, he had a way of dominating every conversation he took part in. He was more than progressive: He was a liberal firebrand. Phillip had a younger brother, John, who was equally brilliant and intense. The year after Phillip went to Congress, John was elected to the California State Assembly. Later he, too, became a member of Congress, and San Francisco was magnificently represented by the Burton brothers.

Shortly before he was elected to the Assembly, Phillip had married Sala Galante, a Polish Jewish woman whose family had immigrated to the United States during World War II. Sala was divorced, with a young daughter. She was as soft-spoken as Phillip was loud. The two met at a Young Democrats event, and when they married, it was during another YD meeting—to which they returned after the wedding! You couldn't be part of Democratic politics in San Francisco without knowing the Burtons. Over time, Sala and I became close friends.

After Sala asked me to run, the first person I talked to was Paul. "Yes, you should run, and you'll win it," he said, "but only if you want to do it, not because other people think it's a good idea." As usual from my husband, excellent advice.

Paul and I had to seriously evaluate the impact my running for office would have on our family. We knew that campaigns are brutal in what people say and that winning means great sacrifice for the family personally and professionally. The question was "Is it worth it?"

From my own experience and from observing the careers of many of my women colleagues, depending on one's own personal situation, the answer is yes. The opportunity to bring women's voices to the table in greater numbers must be exploited. The real question is how long do you stay. But should you go? The answer is yes. It is worth it for you, and necessary for the country.

We then talked to our children, and they were very excited. My greatest concern, however, was our youngest daughter, Alexandra. The only one of our five children born in California, she was going into her senior year in high school and was the only one still living at home. Alexandra was in some ways our most challenging child. As an adolescent, she was a rebel, which she demonstrated in her attire, among other things. She picked up clothes for a dollar in Haight-Ashbury, men's shirts from the 1960s and whatever else appealed to her. She wore black high-top sneakers, even at Thanksgiving dinner, and when several of the parents asked her, "Alexandra, is that what all the young people are wearing now?" she replied, "Yes, and soon you'll be wearing them, too."

Sure enough, when these same people attended a charity fashion show a few months later they noted in amazement that the models were indeed wearing black high-top sneakers.

I thought I owed it to my free-spirited youngest child to be sure I knew how she felt. After all, the possibility of my taking on the large and unanticipated job of campaigning for Congress—not to mention the possibility of actually having to serve—would have a bigger impact on her than on her siblings.

"Alexandra," I said, "you know that Sala wants me to run for her seat. I know the timing is not ideal. A year from now, when you're in college, would be much better. I would leave San Francisco on Mondays and come back Thursday nights. I know this is a big deal, so if you don't want me to do it, I won't. I promise you I'll be very happy either way."

I didn't have to wait long for an answer. Alexandra said, *"Mother, get a life!"*

I was trying so hard to be a great mom, giving my little heartfelt speech, and my youngest put it all in perspective for me in three words—"get a life"—and so I did.

Now that Alexandra had given me her blessing, I spoke to John Burton, who would become my campaign chair; Leo McCarthy, my friend and mentor; Mario Cuomo, who had supported me in my race for DNC Chair; and Senator George Mitchell, for whom I had served as the finance chair of the Democratic Senate Campaign Committee the year before.

Mario Cuomo and George Mitchell, in fact, had been saying that someday I should run for public office. When

I told them that Sala wanted me to run for her seat, they were both very encouraging.

The man I wanted to hire as my campaign manager, Clint Reilly, quickly brought me back to earth. A battle-hardened veteran of many campaigns, he had cross-indexed the whole city and taken polls to reinforce his unsurprising conclusion: A gay man would beat me.

My major opponent was, indeed, a gay man—a County Supervisor. "He will win," my would-be campaign manager said, "because the gay vote in San Francisco is huge." He cited two other strong Democratic candidates who were running, an African American woman and an Irish American man. They were County Supervisors, too.

"You'll come in second," Clint said. "You probably can't win because no woman has ever gotten the votes in the parts of the city where you would need to come in first."

I heard him out. "You know what?" I said. "If your numbers are correct, I can definitely win. First of all, I will out-organize my opponents. Second, there's one thing you aren't recognizing about that part of town. They're Italian American. And they are going to vote for me."

"You're right," he replied. "There's a chance they'll vote for you."

Clint signed on and planned a campaign that connected my Democratic Party leadership with Democratic legislative accomplishments.

We had just six weeks to create an organization, marshal my endorsements, and raise a million dollars—all of this at the same time we were mourning Sala's death. Our old slogan, "Organize, don't agonize," helped keep us focused.

John Burton, who had agreed to co-chair my campaign, said, "Sala was brilliant. She endorsed someone who could raise a million dollars in six weeks." I was fortunate because there were many people in California and all over the country who supported my candidacy.

I was different in those days: a dedicated Democrat and an effective party organizer, but not in any way a public person. Selling myself as a candidate was hard, but if you're asking people to support you in any endeavor, you have to make the case for yourself. Running for Congress is not for the faint of heart.

Fortunately for me, Paul was very supportive on the home front. While it was not required by law that we live in the Congressional district—and it was just a matter of a few blocks—we anticipated that not living in the district could be a political liability for my candidacy.

This time it was Paul's turn to move.

He immediately started a search for a new house. He did all the legwork and showed me about five places, and we settled on one. While I was campaigning, he moved our entire family in practically no time.

My day often began at 5:00 A.M. to work the bus stops, and continued late into the night. When I wasn't campaigning, I was strategizing. Once when I was away for the entire day I came home to a surprise party—a fundraiser put on by our friends in our Presidio Terrace home—and the house had not one stick of furniture in it (*really,* this time). There was nothing there except our piano and hundreds of people. Everything else had been moved.

Congressional seats like Sala's don't open up very often, so I knew it would be a fierce competition.

"What am I going to do when they start attacking me?" I asked John Burton. "How will I neutralize that?"

"What are you thinking?" John replied impatiently. "They're not going to attack you. You'll probably be an asterisk in the first poll."

Strangely enough, this was not the case. I'll never forget the big smile on John's face when he told me the first poll gave me 29 percent of the vote and my next-closest opponent 14 percent. The other candidates stood at 11 and 9 percent.

It turned out that being new was an advantage over my better-known opponents. I was not part of the elected establishment. My statement at the time about my opponents was, "Apparently, to know them is not to love them"—and clearly, that was the case.

The most important factor in my favor was that Sala had endorsed me, and John had sent out a mailer saying that she had done so. I had assured her that I would give it my very best effort, and it was a promise I was determined to keep.

One of my most enthusiastic supporters was Paul's mother. Nana organized her friends into the "Nana Brigade" to campaign on my behalf. They made endless phone calls and sent postcards to the eight thousand Italian Americans in the district.

Nana's friends also gave me some advice about approaching bingo players at Catholic church halls. Most politicians would speak too long, which irritated the players, who were passionately devoted to their pastime.

I would go in and quickly say, "Hello, I'm Nancy Pelosi, and I'm running for Congress. I see that you're busy, and I don't want to delay your game. I hope you will remember me on Election Day, April 7." (It's always important to mention the date of the election.) And then, before I would leave, I would make sure to sweeten the pot. Sweetening the pot always got a big cheer.

Once the polls showed my opponents that I was in the lead, the attacks came fast and furious. Just as in the DNC race, some of the worst things said about me came from people I knew well—friends for whom I had hosted events in my home. Some of it was downright cruel. But this time I was ready.

People kept saying to me, "I can't believe how you stay above the fray." My answer was, "I got my knocks early, and I know now why I went through that. These people are not going to throw me off my game."

And they didn't.

I'm sure that my children and Paul must have taken great personal offense at every attack, but they decided not to burden me with their feelings. Some of my friends, on the other hand, would call me and say, "You'll never believe the mailer I got against you! It's horrible!"

I'd say, "Don't bog me down with that. If you have a problem with it, go out and recruit volunteers and raise money for my campaign."

As friends, they wanted to protect me, but what I needed most was for them to join us in the trenches.

Some of the accusations made about me were actually funny. According to one series of mailers and advertisements, I was a "dilettante." Many people seemed confused by the word. Some seemed to think it somehow meant "debutante."

I looked pretty old, they thought, to be a debutante!

It backfired on my opponents, because the response from many voters was, "Is that the worst they can come up with?"

My children had no doubt whatsoever that I would win, and they all volunteered to work on my campaign; Christine actually took a semester off from Georgetown to help.

Many people assumed that I still had little ones at home. I was asked over and over again, "Who is taking care of your children?" My answer was, "My children are grown and are taking care of *me*." In 1987, even among the progressives who wanted to see more women in public office, some were uneasy with the idea of a mother running for Congress who still had little children at home.

Another double standard is the way in which the press—and the public, too—examines a woman candidate's clothing and hair down to the millimeter. My male opponents received no such scrutiny.

One day I happened to be wearing the best suit I'd ever owned—one that Paul had bought as a special birthday present—while campaigning. Trailed by newspaper and television journalists, I walked into a beauty shop looking for votes. The first words came from a lady who pointed at me and said, *"I know that suit!"*

My heart sank. *Oh, my God,* I thought. *She knows my suit.*

My mind was racing. And this dear lady would not be quiet. "I'd know that suit anywhere!" she exclaimed. "I *love* that suit!"

I could imagine the headlines: "Pelosi Campaigns in Designer Suit."

"I'd know it anyplace!" the lady continued. But then she added, "It's my favorite pattern. Simplicity 124!"

Thank you, God!

John Burton and I had created a true grassroots operation, consisting of hundreds of supporters. I've been asked, where did all of these people come from? Many had been volunteers during the Democratic National Convention in 1984, when I had served as chair of the Host Committee. To me, each of the volunteers was a VIP, and I had treated them accordingly. Now that I was running for Congress, they were eager to help. I had hundreds of people walking precincts to rally support and turn out the vote for me. I knew from experience that organization would be the key.

I observed this as a little girl, when my father first ran for Mayor of Baltimore. I remember a conversation, early on the morning of Election Day, between my father and my oldest brother, Tommy.

"What do you think?" Tommy asked our father. "How do you think we're going to do?"

And Daddy's reply was, "Let's go to the roof."

From the roof of our house, you could see the central election headquarters. Starting at 5:00 A.M., people were supposed to converge there to get their campaign packets to give to precinct workers in their neighborhoods, who would then go door-to-door to turn out the vote.

So Tommy and Daddy went up to the roof of our house at 245 Albemarle Street, and they saw headlights coming from every direction, converging on election headquarters.

The organization was working.

"I think we are going to give them a good run," Daddy said. And he was right! When the results were in, Daddy had won a hard-fought victory for Mayor.

You have to know how to count the votes—to anticipate how many people will vote for you. And in order to turn out those votes, you have to be organized on every level. This was the D'Alesandro model. It was also the Burton model, and it worked in San Francisco.

Back East, my D'Alesandro family was rooting for me. Throughout my campaign, my father kept saying, "Don't worry about me; I don't need a ticket to your swearing-in, because I can go onto the floor. Former members can go right to the floor."

"Dad," I said, "I haven't won the election yet."

"Well, you work on that," my father said. "But don't worry about a ticket for me."

And—just as he had once taken my brother Tommy to the roof of the Albemarle Street house when he was running for Mayor—my father sent Tommy out to check on my campaign.

Tommy came and realized what a great grassroots operation I had. He saw the huge cadre of volunteers. He understood that it was a real fight in the trenches for the vote. When he called our father, Daddy said, "So how is it? What's her campaign like? Does she have a good organization?"

"Yes," Tommy said. "She's true to her roots. She's going to give them a run. It's just a question of what the other side has."

Indeed it was. A week before the election, we acknowledged the most important D'Alesandro rule of all: Count Your Votes. And so we did a series of calculations based on the expected turnout. If things broke poorly for me—

if my supporters simply didn't turn out on Election Day because they assumed I would definitely win—and the best-case scenario happened for my opponents, I would lose by five hundred to a thousand votes.

So we went that extra mile and pushed for five thousand more Pelosi votes, a number chosen because it would, we hoped, give us a wide, safe margin. Early on, my campaign had hired two former organizers for the United Farm Workers union, Fred Ross Jr. and Marshall Ganz, who expertly built my get-out-the-vote effort. The UFW model is very disciplined and precise, and its founders, Cesar Chavez and Dolores Huerta, were an inspiration to all of us. When volunteers are recruited, they must do everything they agreed to, no matter how small. In the last week, my volunteers went door-to-door one more time.

And it worked.

On Election Day, I won my first Congressional race by just under four thousand votes. My family was thrilled—Paul and our children, Nana and all of my other in-laws, my brothers and their families, and, of course, my parents. I was the first daughter in history to follow her father into Congress. Several times, Daddy expressed astonishment and pride that I had won in a district that was three thousand miles from Baltimore, without using the D'Alesandro name, and nearly forty years after he had served in the House.

And he reminded me that he didn't need a ticket to get on the floor.

I won because I was able to organize in a variety of ways, all of which came together on Election Day. While growing up in a political family was obviously helpful, the organizational skills I developed as a mom were equally important.

As one of my friends once said about me, "I knew she was going places when I would go to her house and see those little children folding their own laundry and organizing it in stacks!"

I was now heading to Congress to serve the people of San Francisco, a city that I had come to love with all my heart. When people asked me what I had learned growing up in Baltimore that prepared me to represent a city as diverse as San Francisco, I explained that the pride I have in my own Italian American heritage makes me appreciate the pride others have in theirs.

San Francisco is blessed with every ethnic group, nationality, religion, and political belief. We take pride in our large gay, lesbian, bisexual, and transgender community. I always say of San Francisco that the beauty is in the mix.

When I return home from Washington I savor the

differences, visiting Chinatown, Japantown, the Mission, the Bayview, and other neighborhoods. Like our nation, we are constantly refreshed by newcomers from across the country and the world.

San Francisco is an entrepreneurial city and a strong union town. It began as a pioneer destination during the Gold Rush and continues in that spirit by promoting community, individual rights, and protection of the environment. For us, these are not issues, they are our values.

San Franciscans lead the way in caring about our families. Every child in San Francisco has health care until twenty-five years of age. We have a living wage, which is higher than the minimum wage. Much of this is thanks to the leadership of Mayor Gavin Newsom, who also has made San Francisco one of the greenest cities in America.

We are a city of hope because we are a city of faith and charity. St. Francis of Assisi is our city's patron saint, and the prayer of St. Francis is our city's anthem:

"Lord, make me a channel of thy peace, where there is darkness may we bring light. Where there is hatred may we bring love, and where there is despair, may we bring hope."

It is that spirit that sent me to Congress, and it is in that spirit, with great gratitude, that I represent the City of St. Francis.

8

A Voice That Will Be Heard

The number one issue for my constituents when I first went to Congress in the late 1980s was AIDS. But I found out almost immediately that others didn't share my concern.

On the day I was sworn in, some of my fellow members had told me, "You're not supposed to say a word. They'll say, 'Do you swear or affirm that you will uphold the Constitution of the United States, from all enemies foreign and domestic . . . so help you God?' And you'll just say yes. That's all. That's the way it's done."

Oh, my, I thought, with some disappointment. *All these people have come from California, from Maryland, from all over to see me sworn in, and I'm not going to say anything? Don't the powers that be know my campaign slogan was "The Voice That Will Be Heard"? How can I not be heard?*

But then, after I took the oath, Jim Wright, the Speaker of the House, who was presiding, graciously said, "Would the gentlewoman from California like to address the House?"

This was, of course, a complete surprise. My fellow members whispered, "Keep it short, really short."

And so I did. "Thank you, Mr. Speaker," I said. "I'm so honored to be here today with my family and with my father, Thomas D'Alesandro, a former member"—they applauded—"and my constituents from the great city of San Francisco, which I'm proud to represent. In the course of my campaign, I promised that when I came to Congress, I would tell you that Sala sent me, and that I came to fight against AIDS."

The members who had told me not to say anything looked stricken. Afterward, on my way in to my first vote, some of them took me aside.

"Why on earth would you want the first thing anybody knows about you to be that your priority is to fight against AIDS?"

"Well, that really is why I came here. It's one of my top priorities." In our district, we had lost hundreds of people already to the disease. We knew the value of community-based initiatives for HIV and AIDS, whether prevention, care, or research for a cure.

It was just stunning to me that they would object to my mentioning one of the greatest health care crises in U.S. history. I thought, *Why would you say that to me? I just got sworn into Congress. And you're telling me that I shouldn't tell people I came here to fight against AIDS?*

Shortly after I became a Member of Congress, Cleve Jones, a leader in the gay and lesbian community in our city, came up with an interesting idea. He wanted to create a quilt composed of patches made by people across America in honor of a family member, friend, or loved one who had died of AIDS. The beauty of the quilt would be the diversity of the patches.

Cleve wanted soon-to-be Mayor Art Agnos, Leo McCarthy, then Lt. Governor, and me to hold a fundraiser in my home to announce the project, which was called the NAMES Project AIDS Memorial Quilt. We agreed. But I also expressed a concern. I told them I had learned to sew when I was a little girl because my mother had insisted on it, but that I didn't sew that much anymore. Furthermore, I didn't know many people who still did.

Cleve insisted that it would be a success, and he was so very right. It is absolutely impossible to talk about the quilt—and, certainly, to see it—without having an emotional response. It was also therapeutic for the loved ones who sewed the patches.

My children and I made one in memory of Susie Piracci, a flower girl at my wedding and the younger sister of my brother Tommy's wife, Margie. Susie died of AIDS, but not before becoming a champion in the fight against the disease, taking her message of prevention to high school classrooms throughout Maryland.

Cleve wanted to have the quilt displayed on the Mall in Washington, D.C. At first the National Park Service said no. Empowered by the support I received from colleagues in Congress, especially from California, we wouldn't take no for an answer.

Then the Park Service told me their approval would require lifting the quilt every twenty minutes for the duration of the weekend in order to aerate the ground underneath. If not, the grass would be harmed. We agreed, recognizing that they were sincere about their concern for the lawn—though I was uncertain if it was their only concern. And Cleve assured them that we would have thousands of volunteers for the entire weekend.

With the assurance that we would lift the quilt every twenty minutes, the Park Service gave their approval. It was a triumphant moment for the cause. Cleve Jones had given America an opportunity to grieve for those who had lost their lives to AIDS. The vast size of the quilt made a statement about the enormous scale of the tragedy. The patches served to memorialize each person individually. We were all overjoyed when the national news showed aerial views of the quilt, and Cleve Jones was named the ABC Newsmaker of the Week.

When I arrived in Congress, I was eager to get on an AIDS health subcommittee. The health subcommittees were highly coveted positions, and I really didn't have much of a chance to be appointed. Fortunately, my colleague from California, Henry Waxman, who was the House's top crusader in the fight against AIDS, generously gave up one of his health assignments so I could serve.

Coming from San Francisco, I was appalled at how openly disrespectful some members of Congress were about people with HIV/AIDS, and even more disturbed that they would take their bigotry to the floor of the House.

Early on, I was watching the floor proceedings from my office when I heard a virulently antigay member from southern California ranting about HIV/AIDS and saying that it was a punishment for sin. I called Barney Frank, Congressman from Massachusetts, and said, "This is terrible! What can we do?"

I must have taken too long to explain my dismay, because Barney made his impatience clear. He said, "Welcome to Congress, Nancy. This is what goes on here. But don't complain to me about it—go out on the floor and respond to him."

His advice sounded familiar: It was what I'd said to friends during my campaign.

Barney gave me another lesson that day: Keep it short when talking to colleagues. Today our phone conversations sound something like this: "Barney? Nancy. Subject: low-income housing. Question: When will your bill be ready?"

We don't even speak in full sentences! It's just topic, question, reaction. His advice has served me well.

Another issue important to my district is human rights, specifically what is happening in China. My district includes San Francisco's famous Chinatown, and many of my constituents were deeply concerned—as was I—when the Chinese government began to crack down on protesters who were demonstrating peacefully in Beijing and throughout China. Huge demonstrations led to the Tiananmen Square massacre, where more than two thousand people who had dared to speak out against the government were killed and many more injured. The massacre was followed by even more suppression and imprisonment of protesters.

All across America, there were rallies supporting the Chinese dissidents. Many students and scholars had come to the United States from China on student visas, and I believed we had a responsibility to protect them. We were aware that the Chinese government was keeping very close tabs on these young people while they were here in America, and that those who demonstrated would face arrest when their visas expired and they returned to China.

I fought very hard in Congress to allow these young people to stay in the United States until it was safe for them to return home. We wrote legislation to protect them, which passed in both the House and Senate. Then President George Herbert Walker Bush vetoed the bill. We overrode his veto in the House, and it went over to the Senate. The President did not want to sign the bill. He did not want to offend the Chinese government. And he didn't want us to win. He worked the Senate, even sending handwritten notes to the wives of some Senators to try to get them to encourage their husbands to vote against the override. He met so much resistance, he finally said he would issue an Executive Order requiring exactly what our bill did to protect the Chinese students, but that the bill itself should be defeated. So the veto was not overridden. Time passed, and he did not sign the

Executive Order. We believed he would never do it, which may well have been his plan.

Supporters of the legislation went to the *Washington Post* with one of the handwritten notes, and they published it. This forced President Bush to finally issue the Executive Order. Working with the Chinese students and scholars has been one of my most rewarding endeavors in Congress.

The following year I went on a human rights trip to China. It was a bipartisan delegation of Members of Congress, including Representatives John Miller and Ben Jones, and outside human rights activists. The Chinese government restricted us to a bus and moved us around Beijing, basically just keeping us away from the place we most wanted to go. Finally, I said I needed to go back to my room. So they took us to our hotel. And then we took a cab to Tiananmen Square.

The press followed. As soon as we got to Tiananmen Square, we unfurled a banner that read, "To Those Who Died For Democracy In China." During our trip, we wore white silk flowers in our lapels as a symbol of our sympathy with democracy advocates in China. We took off the flowers and placed them at the Monument to the People's Heroes.

There were people around us who we had thought

were tourists. When our flowers touched the monument, their walkie-talkies came out. They, and others from the People's Liberation Army, chased us wielding billy clubs. Those who didn't run fast enough were hit. Some of the press people who had followed us were detained and their film or video was confiscated.

Nevertheless, someone's video made it to CNN, and at a banquet that evening, Chinese government officials expressed their displeasure over what we had done. And I made them well aware of mine.

Our voices must always be heard.

The issue of human rights in China and Tibet is still very important to me.

I was pleased that President George W. Bush presented the Congressional Gold Medal to the Dalai Lama at the Capitol in October 2007.

In March 2008, I led a Congressional delegation to India. Part of our mission was to meet with the Dalai Lama in Dharamsala, the headquarters of Tibetan exiles. By co-incidence, our long-planned trip took place just after the largest protests in Tibet in decades, which were followed by an intense crackdown by China.

"Tibet challenges the conscience of the world," I told the audience at a gathering outside the town's main temple. "If freedom-loving people throughout the world do not speak out against China's oppression in China and Tibet, we have lost all moral authority to speak on behalf of human rights anywhere in the world."

During my visit, I thought about Martin Luther King Jr., who had come to India during the Civil Rights Movement to learn about Gandhi's principles of nonviolence. Interestingly, the Sanskrit word *satyagraha,* which means "truth insistence," also became synonymous with "nonviolence." That is what the Civil Rights Movement was about—shining a bright light of truth on the injustice and horror of segregation.

We must also insist upon the truth in exposing human rights abuses. It is said that the most excruciating punishment that can be inflicted on political prisoners is to tell them that no one in the outside world remembers them, knows they're in prison, or cares. My colleagues and I do what we can to let these prisoners know they are not forgotten. In the United States, we keep lists of their names, read them on the floor of the House, and present them whenever we come in contact with Chinese officials. We have worked to free many prisoners who are now in the United States. My great hope is that they can live and speak freely in China and Tibet someday.

Not only did I oppose President George H. W. Bush on his China policy, I strenuously disagreed with Democratic

President Bill Clinton on his trade and human rights policies toward China and Tibet as well. This was difficult because I otherwise greatly supported and admired his leadership. My father faced a similar situation in Congress. Although he was a New Deal Democrat and followed Franklin D. Roosevelt's lead, there was one area in which he disagreed with the administration. Daddy supported an organization called the Bergson Group, which had rallies, pageants, and parades focusing attention on the plight of European Jews during World War II and calling for the establishment of a Jewish state in Palestine, which was not yet the administration's policy. Daddy's activism sprang in part from his early friendships in the Jewish community. As a boy, he had been a *Shabbos goy* and learned Yiddish, and his enthusiasm came from doing what he believed was right.

The American people have spoken out against oppression wherever it occurs in the world—Tibet and the brutal repression of Aung San Suu Kyi in Burma are two current examples. The world has some level of shame that it did not intervene to prevent the slaughter in Rwanda, which makes the genocide in Darfur all the more intolerable. Two years ago I visited Darfur with a delegation of House members. We were horrified by what we saw in refugee camps—one had more than a hundred thousand people living in subhuman conditions. We were told that during the night, fathers were killed, mothers were raped, and children were kidnapped—this is the situation in Darfur.

When we went to Khartoum, the capital of Sudan, to meet with government officials, they denied what we had seen with our own eyes. The international response can be effective only if China is willing to support Security Council actions to end the genocide. So far, they refuse to do so. The Chinese are oppressing Tibetans, bolstering the Burmese junta, and supporting the Sudanese government—and expect world leaders to stand with them at the opening ceremonies of the 2008 Olympics in Beijing.

On some of our dark days in our fight for human rights, my late colleague Tom Lantos, a Holocaust survivor, counseled us that the struggle is a long one and we must have faith that we will succeed—and insist that our voices be heard.

That is why I keep two framed photos next to each other on my desk. One is of the group of us unfurling our banner in Tiananmen Square. The other, given to me by one of my dearest friends in the world, Congresswoman Anna Eshoo, is a framed quote by Mother Teresa: "God does not always expect us to be successful, but He does always expect us to be faithful."

9

"Age Quod Agis":
Do What You Are Doing

When Sala asked me to accept her endorsement to run for her seat, she said to the others in the room, "Nancy is smart, she's tough, she's operational, she's good on the issues." After the meeting, when there were just the two of us, she said, "You've got to be ready. *Are you ready?*"

Although Sala had earlier told me the purpose of the meeting, and had asked me to be prepared with my decision, I was struck by the gravity of the moment and the reality of what it meant in terms of Sala's health, as well as the implications for my life.

But in answer to her question: Yes, I was ready.

And the message I would like to convey sounds simple enough, but there is power in the words: *Be ready.*

It was 1994. I had been in Congress only six years. And a number of members came to me and said, "We want you to run for Speaker."

I thought they were crazy. I said, "Me, run for Speaker? I'm just in my third term!"

They said, "We think the Democrats are going to lose in the House unless we can show that we represent change, and a woman Speaker represents change. You know the issues, you know the politics, and you can help us win the Congressional elections in 1994."

I tried to dampen their enthusiasm, but they were certain the Democrats would lose otherwise.

Soon, some of the people who were close to then-Speaker Tom Foley came to me and said, "You know, you're not doing yourself any good around here by putting out the idea that you might run for Speaker." It was strange to hear them question my loyalty to Tom Foley. I had no interest in running for *any* leadership post, especially that of Speaker.

The House members who approached me in 1994 were right about the grim prospects for the Democrats.

We lost the House and didn't get it back until 2006. Little did I know then that when we did get the House back, I would become Speaker. When I see those former members who encouraged me to run in 1994, they laugh and say, "We started it."

During those twelve years, I focused on deepening my knowledge of a broad range of policy issues and building on the work I had done earlier. I had already served on the Health Subcommittee of the Government Operations Committee, as well as the Banking Committee. It was my privilege to serve on the Appropriations Committee, and to learn from a master, our Chairman, David Obey. I was also fortunate to work with Rosa DeLauro and Nita Lowey on the Labor, Health, and Human Services Subcommittee to promote women's and children's health issues, to increase funding for the battles against breast cancer and HIV/AIDS, and to double the budget of the National Institutes of Health. I also served on the Ethics Committee for seven years, encouraging Congress to live up to the highest ethical standards; and on the Intelligence Committee, where I forged my national security credentials—and where I would become the longest-serving member in Congressional history.

On the political side, the Democrats lost again in 1996 and 1998. In anticipation of the election of 2000, my own supporters outside Congress were frustrated. They said, "We contribute to the Democratic Congressional Campaign Committee—to the candidates of the DCCC's choosing. We give to the party, then they spend it on a plan that you are not a part of. We're not interested in this arrangement."

I desperately believed that the American people would be better off with a Democratic majority. Because I wanted to have a bigger impact on the Congressional campaigns in 2000, I decided to run for Whip, assuming a Democratic victory, which would have created an opening.

Outside of Congress, my supporters were very energized by the idea that I might have a role in leading us to victory.

Inside the Congress, others were less thrilled.

"Who said she could run?" they said.

Who said she could run? That put me into fighting mode. I did not need anyone to tell me I could or could not run.

By running for Whip, I would defy more than two hundred years of men following in each other's footsteps for all of the major leadership positions.

In 2000, I believed that we would be able to get the seven seats we needed to take back the House. As we went into the race, I said to Minority Leader Dick Gephardt, "If you're counting on California for us to win the majority, take it to the bank—we're going to do very well here. All you have to do is come out ahead by two more seats in the rest of the country."

Due to the personal and political efforts of our candidates, the campaigns went beautifully in California. We had the best candidates—Susan Davis, Jane Harman, Mike Honda, Adam Schiff, and Hilda Solis. We had the best communication of message, the best organization, and the best get-out-the-vote plan. We were very focused, and we knew the grassroots in those districts, right down to the last blade of grass.

With the help of Representatives Mike Thompson and Zoe Lofgren, we paid very close attention to the issues and how they played in each section of every district. We had our national message of economic growth and national security. Most important, the candidates had their own messages, specific to the needs of their constituents. And the campaigns were seriously funded. Starting then and continuing to today, I have had the benefit of Brian Wolff's extraordinary political and fundraising talents.

When Election Night came, we won five seats from the Republicans in California. We were ecstatic, and assumed we had taken back the majority.

But we hadn't.

I was in San Francisco that night. We had come in from

the trenches—we'd been working all day—and I held a press conference. We were feeling very confident. As I approached the podium a staff person kept pulling my sleeve. "Hold on," she said. "CNN is saying that the Republicans have retained control of the Congress."

That isn't possible, I thought.

But it turned out that because of Democratic losses elsewhere, we netted exactly *one* seat. In addition to California, the only other House seat we won was in Arkansas, where Mike Ross overtook his opponent largely through his personal effort. It was a shock, to say the least.

Because the Democrats did not regain control of the House in 2000, there was no change of leadership. But then in 2001, David Bonior, the very respected Democratic Whip, announced that he would run for Governor of Michigan, and the position of Whip was finally open. The race was difficult, but I won a strong majority of the House Democrats and became the first woman Whip in Congress.

Each party in the House has a Whip. The origin of the term is not only as people think from "cracking the whip," but also from the British hunt, where a breed of dog called whippets, I am told, was used to keep hunting dogs in line as they chased the fox. My responsibility was to make sure that when the Democratic leader had a bill on the floor, we got the largest possible number of Democrats to vote for it and, we hoped, some Republicans as well. I loved the job, because it brings you in close contact with your fellow members of Congress. You hear their concerns and those of their constituents, and you help shape the legislation to reflect those needs. Our caucus is very diverse—by philosophy, geographic region, generation, gender, race, and ethnicity—making it challenging to forge a strong consensus among members.

I had hoped the Democrats would win in 2004, and that Dick Gephardt, our great Minority Leader, would become Speaker and I would have the privilege of serving under him as the Majority Leader. But the Democrats lost, and the day after the election Dick announced that he was stepping aside to run for President. While I was sad about our election loss and that Dick would not be Speaker, my "organize, don't agonize" mentality came into play. I had to make an instant decision to run for the top spot. While my colleagues had elected me Whip, the question was, would they give me the top position of leader? I would soon find out.

I immediately went into action and called over 150 Democratic members to personally ask them for their vote, and in twenty-four hours I had the votes I needed.

And I was ready to be leader.

This new role could not have been possible without the support of my family.

The initial plan, when I first came to Washington, was to serve five terms in the House (assuming, as I hoped, that my constituents would reelect me), then move on with my life. Ten years seemed like a very long time. Now I have been in Congress for twenty-one.

I knew from the beginning that Paul was never going to live in Washington. He deserves a lot of credit for supporting my career, especially since it's not what he bargained for when we got married.

Fortunately, he has a number of interests besides his business. He has always been an enthusiastic, natural athlete (while I am anything but) and can't live without his exercise—tennis, golf, and cycling. He loves the arts, especially the performing arts. In support of the scholarship program at Town School for Boys, where our son had gone to grade school, Paul became involved in parents' school plays—eleven plays in eleven years. He was a wonderful Henry Higgins, Harold Hill, Will Parker, and Buffalo Bill, to name a few. And for years, he served on the board of the Convent of the Sacred Heart, our daughters' school.

For over twenty years I have gone home to San Francisco almost every weekend to be with Paul and to spend time with my constituents. I've flown across the country fifteen hundred times, maybe more. Washington is the place I work; San Francisco is where I live.

Everyone can agree that time with loved ones—as well as time away from them—must be spent wisely.

Politics can be an insatiable beast and very demanding of one's time. I frequently tell my colleagues that we must always appreciate the value of our days with family and friends. They are the source of our strength and we wouldn't be in Congress without them. Benefiting from our time with loved ones requires focus—putting our work on the shelf. Recreation is essential to our sanity. To "recreate" is to "re-create" our energy, our spirit, and our friendships.

So whether it is work or play, helping around the house or entertaining the kids, focus on it.

Remember the Latin phrase "Age quod agis"—do what you are doing.

10

Think Outside the Beltway

Representing California in Congress, I was always invigorated by the fresh new ideas of my constituents. Then I would go back inside the Beltway and hit a wall, because Washington has been the city of the status quo.

Long before I became the Democratic Leader, I looked for ways to be entrepreneurial and to find innovative solutions to difficult problems. One of my major legislative accomplishments was finding a way to turn the Presidio from an Army post into a national park.

The Federal government closed the Presidio in the late 1980s. The Base Realignment and Closure Commission made that decision, even though its members never walked the grounds. They didn't understand that they never could have sold it, as they had assumed, for a billion dollars because the people of San Francisco would never allow the Presidio to be developed.

Fortunately, when Phillip Burton was in Congress, he respected the vision of environmental activists Dr. Ed Wayburn and Amy Meyer, and established the Golden Gate National Recreation Area. Phillip quietly had written into law that when the Presidio was no longer needed by the Department of Defense, it would become part of the GGNRA. No one paid attention at the time because it had seemed so unlikely.

Then the Presidio closed, and the sparks began to fly. The federal government still thought they could sell the land for development. Some people in the community wanted the U.S. Government to take it over and to pay the tens of millions of dollars it would cost each year to maintain it as a park, draining millions from an already meager National Park budget.

I joined those who were looking for a new approach. Jim Harvey, a respected businessman in San Francisco who, along with his wife, Charlene, was an enthusiastic environmentalist, took the lead in forming the Presidio Council. Composed of representatives from the environmental, business, and nonprofit worlds, the Presidio

Council developed several models, which resulted in a proposal for a public-private partnership.

The Presidio Trust legislation that I authored was entrepreneurial in its thinking and bipartisan in its support, both inside and outside Congress. Senators Barbara Boxer and Dianne Feinstein in the Senate, along with George Miller and our early champion, Jack Murtha, in the House—as well as House Republican Ralph Regula—were all instrumental in its passage.

Because of the leadership of Toby Rosenblatt, the first chair of the Presidio Trust, we are on schedule to meet our goal in 2013, when the Presidio will no longer be dependent on Federal funds and will meet its full operating cost. The Presidio Trust stands today as a model of fresh thinking, and confirms my belief that new, outside-the-Beltway strategies were needed in Washington and could be made to work. Many members want to copy our Presidio Trust model, and what I tell them is that it can't work everywhere. What can be copied is the entrepreneurial spirit that created it.

I was determined to apply these same outside-the-Beltway ideas to help the Democratic Party regain control of Congress.

Tom Daschle and I, as Senate and House Democratic Leaders, had already been discussing the possibility of reaching beyond Washington for advice. But Tom, unfortunately for our country, was one of those who lost in the 2004 elections. Harry Reid became the new Senate Democratic Leader, and together we continued the quest.

"The inside-the-Beltway crowd is failing to understand what is happening in this country," I told my colleagues. So we went to leaders in the high-tech industry and in all aspects of marketing and presentation. "Help us establish ourselves," we said, "exactly the way you would establish a brand."

They wanted to help, but they said, "We can't until you know who you are."

Well, we did know, but it was necessary for us to sharpen our priorities, and it was difficult to do so with more than 250 Democrats in the House and Senate and so many excellent ideas. Distilling these recommendations down to six principles required many hours of meetings. In the House, John Cullinane, a friend of Congressman Ed Markey, led some of our discussions. The result was our new Partnership for America's Future, with our six priorities.

We told our marketing experts about our plan, and their answer was blunt.

"Your six ideas are very good, but timing is everything. If you go forward with them now, President Bush can crush you right under his heel. He has the bully pulpit. He is the President of the United States, you're the minority. You have so little power. You can't compete unless you take him down a few pegs first. That's the way it's done in the private sector."

Even though the people we had consulted with had never worked together before, they were unanimous in their response.

First, you must take down the ratings of your opposition.

Second, you must differentiate yourselves from them.

And third, only when the time is right do you present your platform.

In that order.

So we had our strategy—and a gift from the White House: At precisely this point, President Bush decided he wanted to privatize Social Security.

In January 2005, the newly reinaugurated President was at 58 percent in the polls and 60 percent of America's seniors agreed with his new ideas for "saving" Social Security. No one was clear what those ideas were, mind you, but they sounded good. The Bush Administration was very talented at coming up with names for projects that were the polar opposite of their intentions. "Saving Social Security" meant undermining and unraveling

Social Security. They counted on the American people not paying attention to the details.

So now we had 60 percent of America's seniors against us.

Harry Reid and I had to go to our caucuses. I said to my colleagues in the House: "If we, as the Democratic Party, cannot defend Social Security, we belong in the dustbin of history. The President is challenging our value system. He is challenging who we are. And we have to fight him in a very unconventional way: We have to take his plan down. In order to do so, it is essential that we keep the focus on *his* plan."

President Bush's misleading statements about Social Security were fighting words to me. As the daughter of Tommy D'Alesandro, a New Deal Democrat who named one of his sons Franklin Roosevelt D'Alesandro, I felt especially protective of the legacy of Secretary of Labor Frances Perkins, a woman in FDR's cabinet who proposed Social Security. I was grateful to be working alongside Harry Reid, who, as a champion of America's working families, was determined to save Social Security. Harry Reid's strength was essential to our success.

Many Democrats thought we should come up with a rival plan. Harry and I responded, "Social Security *is* our plan. The only way we can beat President Bush is to focus on the shortcomings of *his* plan."

The other key element of our strategy was to go outside of Washington. House and Senate Democrats held more than a thousand town hall meetings on the issue, all around the country. President Bush announced that he would go to 60 cities in 60 days to push for his plan. My response was, "I wish you would go to 120 cities in 120 days, and I'll buy you the ticket. Everywhere you go, Democrats will be there, to inoculate against your message and to educate the public about your plans to privatize Social Security."

In spite of repeated criticisms from the inside-the-Beltway crowd that we should have our own plan, our strategy worked.

We were able to say, "We have a plan. It's called Social Security. The President has a plan. It's called privatization of Social Security." This was the essential contrast we wanted to make clear. Everywhere the President went, he was clobbered at the grassroots level. The numbers were starting to show that senior citizens and others were beginning to agree with us. We were gaining ground.

Harry Reid and I began to sense that victory was possible. But I said, "If we win on this, we can't just take this issue off the table. We must create a two-pronged attack."

Harry and I and the Democratic leadership began to discuss not only the Social Security fight but also what we called the Republicans' "culture of corruption, cronyism, and incompetence," which was fueled by a series of scandals involving Republicans.

Then, in August 2005, came Hurricane Katrina, which was not only a disaster for those impacted directly but also a moral challenge for our entire nation. How could people be left helpless for such a long period of time?

As the floodwaters still threatened the Gulf States, Harry Reid and I, as the Democratic leaders of the Senate and House of Representatives, and the Republican leaders went to meet with the President.

The President briefed us and cautioned against any Congressional criticism or investigation into the Katrina response; that, he said, could wait until later.

"That may be, Mr. President, but what you have to do immediately is fire Michael Brown," I said.

"Why would I do that?" the President asked.

"Because of all the things that didn't go right last week," I said.

"What didn't go right last week?" the President asked. He still believed that Michael Brown—"Brownie"—was doing "a heck of a job." I added that Michael Brown did not have the credentials or the judgment to head FEMA.

When I met the press outside the White House, all I said was, "I suggested to the President that he fire Michael Brown."

"And what did the President say?" the reporters asked.

All I told the reporters was, "The President said, 'Thank you for your suggestion.'" Which he truly did say.

The next day President Bush went on a rant of misrepresentations about what was going on in the Gulf region. Hours later, I was talking to the press and they asked me again, "What was it the President said when you asked him about firing Michael Brown?"

This time I told them: "The President said, 'Why would I do that? What didn't go right last week?' This President is in denial. He is therefore dangerous."

The White House response was to deny that the conversation had ever taken place. Probably because I had witnesses, including two Republican leaders, they finally admitted that it had occurred.

Meanwhile, the Democrats had successfully pulled back the curtain to reveal the Republicans' culture of corruption, cronyism, and incompetence, and the President's approval rating dropped to 38 percent.

Soon came the time for differentiation: We spelled out

how our proposals and legislation were different from theirs. We *defined* ourselves, which was part two of our strategy.

Only as the midterm elections of 2006 approached did we announce our "New Direction—Six for '06" platform:

- Real Security: at Home and Overseas
- Prosperity: Better American Jobs, and Better Pay
- Opportunity: College Access for All
- Energy Independence
- Affordable Health Care
- Honest Leadership and Open Government

Now people were paying attention. To have revealed our platform earlier would have been a mistake.

As we did our policy work, Rahm Emanuel, as chair of the Democratic Congressional Campaign Committee, did the politics. I chose him to lead the effort because he is a master of political campaigns and because as a policy person he understood how urgent it was to win.

And in November 2006, we reaped the reward. We took back the Congress for the American people. Our outside-the-Beltway strategy had worked. We had looked for a new approach and found it.

More important, we could see it through because our Congressional colleagues trusted the strategy.

To succeed, you can't simply dust off old plans and try harder. As we demonstrated with the Presidio and with "Six for '06," sometimes it is necessary to turn your thinking upside down. Sometimes you need to bring in new people to go in a New Direction.

PART THREE

KNOW YOUR POWER

11

A Seat at the Table

At the beginning of my first year as a leader in Congress, I had an extraordinary experience. It occurred during my first meeting at the White House as part of the Democratic leadership.

I had attended many meetings at the White House before, as a member of the Intelligence Committee and the Appropriations Committee, but when I walked into the room on that January day in 2002, I realized this was unlike any other meeting I had ever been to at the White House.

In fact, it was unlike any meeting *any* woman had ever been to at the White House.

When the door closed behind me, I saw that it was the

President and the leadership—both Democratic and Republican—at the table. Certainly, many respected women had attended cabinet meetings, but they had been there as the President's appointees. This was different. I was there because I was an elected leader of the House Democrats, and I could speak with that independence.

The President, always gracious, welcomed me as a new member of the leadership. As he began the discussion, I suddenly felt crowded in my chair. It was truly an astonishing experience, as if Susan B. Anthony, Elizabeth Cady Stanton, Lucretia Mott, Alice Paul, and all the other suffragettes and activists who had worked hard to advance women in government and in life were right there with me. I was enthralled by their presence, and then I could clearly hear them say:

"At last we have a seat at the table."

After a moment, they were gone.

My first thought was, *We want more—more women and minorities to have seats at the table.*

My second thought was, *What an enormous responsibility, not only to those who came before me but also to the young women who will follow.*

I was standing on the shoulders of all these icons from the past and on those of my contemporaries who gave me guidance when I came to Congress.

When I arrived in 1987, only a small fraction of the representatives were women, but the few who were there generously shared their knowledge and political wisdom. First among them was the elegant and politically astute Congresswoman Lindy Boggs of Louisiana, who had been elected to succeed her husband, Hale Boggs, the Democratic Whip of the House, after his tragic death in a plane crash. Lindy was reelected eight times, representing New Orleans from 1973 to 1991. Later, she would serve as United States Ambassador to the Vatican.

Lindy taught me to think differently. I remember telling her that I thought I had too many opportunities, that perhaps I should give up one of my positions. This was prior to my election to Congress, when I was chair of the 1984 Democratic National Convention Host Committee, and also chaired the committee that enforced the delegate selection rules.

In her wonderful southern accent, she said, "Darlin', no man would ever, ever have that thought."

And then she gave me a significant piece of advice.

"Nancy," she said, "know thy power."

Know your power.

I had power in my hands and I should use it. Lindy's words had an enormous impact on me.

There were other women who inspired me as well,

among them Patsy Mink, Pat Schroeder, and Barbara Kennelly. Patsy was the first Asian American woman in Congress and author of the Title IX amendment to the Education Act, guaranteeing gender equality for girls in athletics and academics. Progressive in her politics and deadly in debate, she took her opponents' arguments apart with strength in her voice and a sparkle in her eye.

Pat Schroeder, of Colorado, was perhaps the bravest woman in Congress. She worked tirelessly for the passage of the Family and Medical Leave Act. Year after year, she fought for the passage of the bill in the House, as did Christopher Dodd in the Senate. But President George H. W. Bush wouldn't sign it. The bill finally was signed into law by President Clinton.

Barbara Kennelly of Connecticut was the first woman to serve on the House Committee on Intelligence. Barbara and I had both grown up in political families—her father, John M. Bailey, had been Chairman of the Democratic National Committee, and was a powerhouse in the Kennedy-Johnson years. We had another shared experience as well: Barbara and I both graduated from Trinity College.

The work of these and other women in Congress helped pave the way for a woman Speaker. They had all broken new ground, and did, to quote Lindy, "know their power"—and used it. There was a sisterhood among us that made the quality of our leadership far outstrip the quantity of women members in Congress.

Nothing has been more wholesome for the politics and the government of our country than the increased participation of women. I hope more women will become involved in electoral politics, whether it is to vote, to campaign for a candidate or a cause, or to run for office themselves. Twenty-two percent of elected officials in the world are women. In the United States, it is only 17 percent.

We want more—in the United States and the world!

Every issue today is a woman's issue—the defense of our country, our economy, education, health care, energy, and protecting the environment. To get more women into public office we must get more women involved in politics. What people don't realize is that even a small amount of time volunteering can make a difference. Can you make a few phone calls? Can you lend your home? Help write press releases? Work for what you believe in, whether it's on a local, state, or national level. That's what I did.

Our daughter Christine remembers leafleting with me when she was a toddler. As my children grew older and we hosted political functions at home, they loved it. To them, it was a big party. Even when the children were small, they enjoyed putting out the hors d'oeuvres, helping set the table, and serving at political events.

When they were older and capable of doing more, they helped with the mailings. Our cheerful assembly line often sang while they worked. One of their favorites was a spirited rendition of "He's Got the Whole World in His Hands." They changed the words to describe the task they were doing: "He's got the stuffers and the sealers in his hands. . . ." The rewards were pizza and ice cream, and soon we had the neighborhood's children as part of our assembly line.

Whatever you can do, just do it. Don't overstate what you will deliver, and always complete the task agreed to.

But get involved, for the future—for your children and grandchildren. For women and girls.

Over and over, young women ask me, "How did you raise five children and go to Congress?" I did it sequentially. I am in awe of the young women who come to Congress while they're still having babies and raising small children. Arriving at a younger age allows them to reach a higher level of success here much sooner than I did. It enables young mothers to be a voice for their generation and to bring their perspective on the issues. I learn from them every day.

Whatever their goals in life may be, women can draw strength and confidence from recognizing that there is nothing more important than investing time and love in the next generation as a mother, an aunt, or a mentor.

When I was a full-time mom and housewife, there was a joke circulating that if society started calling us "domestic engineers," maybe the work we did would be recognized for its true value. It always made me sad when I heard women reply to the question "What do you do?" by saying, "I'm just a housewife." *Just a housewife?*

My message to women is to place a higher value on the experience of being a mother and homemaker. Raising children is saving the world, one child at a time.

There are other obstacles still to be overcome by women to make life better for our daughters and granddaughters, and for our sons and grandsons. For our society to benefit from the full contribution of women at home and at work we must make a national decision to expand access to quality childcare. Quality childcare is the missing link in the chain of progress for women and families. We must make it a priority, and then we will have many more seats at the table.

12

There Is No Secret Sauce

I n 2006, after twelve long years, Congress finally returned to Democratic control. The people had spoken, loud and clear, and it was time for a change. We now
had a majority.

And I became the first woman to hold the position of
Speaker of the House.

The Constitution states that the Speaker is next in
line to the President, after the Vice President. People in
Washington often refer to the "awesome power" of the
Speaker because the position allows you to set the agenda
for the House of Representatives. The Speaker has a great
deal of discretion over appointment to committees, which

bills go to the House floor, and what is contained in legislation.

Immediately after the election, with the help of my colleagues, we put together an agenda for the first one hundred hours of the new session.

Not the first one hundred days—the first one hundred *hours*.

The message we wanted to send to the American people is that we were acting upon the issues that were relevant to their lives, and in a way that leapt over the old ways of passing legislation.

Working with the Democratic leadership—Majority Leader Steny Hoyer; Whip Jim Clyburn; Rahm Emanuel, Chair of the Caucus, and John Larson, Vice Chair; Xavier Becerra, Chris Van Hollen, George Miller, Rosa DeLauro, Charlie Rangel, John Dingell, and our other chairs—we beat our one-hundred-hour goal. From day one, Louise Slaughter, chair of the Rules Committee, kept us on track.

Recognizing our responsibility to protect the American people, and honoring our promise to the 9/11 families, in our first act of Congress we passed House Resolution 1, enacting the 9/11 Commission Recommendations. We passed our Six for '06 agenda: legislation that raised the minimum wage, made college more affordable, promoted stem cell research, repealed subsidies for big oil, and initiated the strongest ethics reform in the history of the Congress.

It would take many more months to get these bills through the Senate, but our initiatives passed with strong bipartisan support, and most were signed into law by President Bush.

Since I first arrived in Congress, I have tried to be an agent of change. Now that I am Speaker, I am using the power of my office to try to jolt Congress out of old ways of thinking, as we did with our agenda for the first one hundred hours. Sometimes it is necessary to disrupt the status quo, especially in a tradition-bound institution such as Congress.

Dr. Clayton Christensen, in his books *The Innovator's Dilemma* and *The Innovator's Solution,* has written of the need for disruption in the world of business. He speaks of how some large corporations become too big and stuck in their ways to stay innovative. Then along comes a company that is more fresh, agile, and resilient, leaving the old business models in the dust.

That is the tradition of our country. Our Founders were disrupters—magnificent disrupters. Martin Luther King Jr.

was a disrupter, as were the suffragettes. It is the American way. The change that resulted from these leaders has made our country greater. How can we follow their lead?

One way in Congress was to reverse the old-boy system, which, to my delight, we have done. In the past, there was a tradition where most of the very senior members known as the old bulls wouldn't even bother to learn the names of the freshmen until they had been re-elected at least once. That is now over. We have moved freshmen to the forefront, giving them top legislation and allowing them important opportunities to be heard. In the past, it would have taken them a long time to reach that level.

When I speak to the freshman class, I tell them that when the new Congress comes in, we say, "Here they are, the fresh recruits, the reinvigoration of the Congress. Every two years, as our Founders intended, there is a new crop." We should listen to them and nurture the talent, creativity, and energy of the new members, not hold them back, which was how it was done for generations.

Some of my colleagues and I look at the freshmen and wonder, *Who among you will be a leader in this body? Who will go to the Senate, be a governor—or, like my father, become a big-city mayor? And who among you may be President of the United States?*

I also think, *And who among you will be disrupters? Because that is what our country needs.*

By electing a woman Speaker, my colleagues turned the old system upside down. In order to understand why we have never had a woman Speaker before, it is necessary to understand the culture of Congress. When I arrived at the Capitol there were 20 women out of 435 representatives. Twenty-one years later, there are 74 women (54 Democrats and 20 Republicans). We want more!

In 1987, Congress was still very much a men's club—or a boys' club, however you want to think of it. The tone had been set in the nineteenth century, and the whiff of old-boy politics still lingered. Cigarette and cigar smoke choked the air. One of my first acts as Speaker was to ban smoking in the Capitol, thereby signaling a change in the atmosphere.

Women and newcomers in Congress, no matter how experienced, had been treated with the same dismissive attitude by the old bulls—except for women it went on for a much longer time.

This is the mystique of the old guard: that somehow, just by donning a man's suit, they became part of a private club that made them infallible. I called it "The Secret Sauce Club." Their message was, "Only we know the secret sauce for success; you don't, and you never will."

But once you've been there for a while—whether it's in Congress, a corporation, a boardroom, or a campus—you find out the truth.

Message to America's daughters: There is no secret sauce.

It's going to take a little more time—and a little more disruption—before the secret sauce attitude completely disappears. But we have reason to be optimistic. Young women today have a sense of confidence that was unusual in my youth. They simply will not be trivialized. Everyone knows there will be many more women in leadership positions in every arena, whether it's in government, business, education, or health care, and that bodes well for the future.

It was hard to imagine, but the sexist atmosphere had actually improved by the time I got to Washington. One Congresswoman from an earlier era recalls walking into her first committee assignment only to be told by the chairman, "I don't want any more broads here."

In 1973, when Pat Schroeder was appointed to the Armed Services Committee, the chairman would not allow her a place to sit. She had to share a single chair—literally—with Ron Dellums, the first African American Congressman to serve on the committee. As Pat wrote in her memoir, they both sat "cheek to cheek" on one chair. Ron Dellums went on to become the chair of the Armed Services Committee and Pat, with her strong national security credentials, to become an icon of women in politics.

Much of the change that finally occurred was due to strides made by women. But some credit also goes to some of the men who came into Congress in the post-Watergate years. This new generation of men was not interested in being part of the old order. Even so, they had their moments.

On Tuesday evenings, I would often have dinner with a group of members of Congress. Usually I went with Barbara Boxer, who helped me the most when I came to Congress, Barbara Kennelly, and several male colleagues. We had many lively debates, and one thing was clear to us: The men never turned and asked, "What do you think?"

Never.

The two Barbaras and I didn't care one bit. We would just chime in if we wanted to. But one night, for some reason, one of our male colleagues brought up the topic of childbirth. Probably a friend or staffer was having a baby.

Before we knew it, all the men were discussing *their experiences with childbirth.*

The first one said, "God, when I had my first, I had the green gown on but they wouldn't let me in the room. . . ."

Next my friend Marty Russo said, "I had a camera, but when I saw it happening, I said, 'Oh, God, let me out of here'. . . ."

Another one said, "Oh, [expletive], I thought I was going to faint. . . ."

Meanwhile, we women were sort of elbowing each other, trying not to laugh. We were all thinking, *Well, surely* now *they'll ask us.*

It never happened. Eleven childbirths among us, and not once did it occur to the men that we might have something to contribute on the subject, or that perhaps we wanted to *change* the subject. They didn't have a clue.

On another occasion, some time later, we were having dinner at Pete Stark's house and the topic of conversation was the Constitution. Don Edwards, who had been the floor leader of the Equal Rights Amendment and who hadn't been at the previous dinner, turned to me and said, "Nancy, what do you think?"

And I said, "Don, thank you so much for asking me what I think! How refreshing!" He was surprised, and asked what I meant. So I retold the childbirth story, and he was astonished. But the best part was that all those same men—the guilty parties—were there as well. And they claimed it never happened.

"We would never do that!" they said.

They didn't even *know* how clueless they were. They didn't have a clue that they didn't have a clue!

But they had not intended to offend us, and we didn't take offense. We had made our point, and that was enough. I had decided, long before, that I didn't come to Congress to change the attitudes of men. I came to change the policies of our country. If some of the men's attitudes changed because they respected the women members, that was fine. But it wasn't my objective. And although I always ask all of my colleagues their opinions, this much I can promise: As the first woman Speaker of the House, I won't be asking these men for their thoughts about childbirth. I think I have that covered.

Having said that, I am proud of my colleagues in the House. By electing a woman Speaker, they have brought us closer to the ideal of equality that is America's heritage and its hope.

13

Remember When You Used to Cook?

Regardless of your chosen path in life, there are several qualities that are needed to succeed, and one that I recommend most heartily is to be able to laugh at yourself.

I can always count on my daughter Alexandra to assist me in that capacity. One day, out of the blue, she said, "Mother, I'm really proud of you because you are a pioneer." It brought a smile to my face.

I said, "Oh, that's so nice of you to say, Alexandra. Am I a pioneer because I'm a woman Member of Congress?"

"No," she said. "Because remember when you used to cook, and then you stopped? Well, now hardly anybody cooks, but you were among the first to stop."

I admit that after cooking meals for five children for twenty years, I had started to pick up more prepared food. *Remember when you used to cook?* With these words, Alexandra took me out of the kitchen and hailed me as a pioneer.

Another time I was brought down to earth was two days after my first election to Congress. I went into a stationery store to buy thank-you notes to send to people who had helped me win. A woman working behind the counter called out, "I know who you are!"

Well, I thought, *I've only been a Congresswoman-elect for two days and look at this! A constituent recognizes me already!*

I was feeling pretty pumped up when the woman added, "You're Barbara Boxer!"

As complimented as I was to be mistaken for Barbara, who is a very special person to my family and me, and a great leader in Congress, I was a bit deflated that I hadn't been recognized.

"Thank you, but no, I'm not," I said.

"Yes, you are!" she insisted.

"No, I'm not," I declared. "I'm Nancy Pelosi."

The woman behind the counter said the most unbelievable thing. "Are you sure?" she asked.

Are you sure?

"Yes, I'm sure."

Barbara and I have been mistaken for each other so often during the past twenty years that we've both finally given up trying to convince people that they have us mixed up. We've learned it's better to simply say, "Thank you."

When I first arrived in Washington, the Capitol Police did not know who I was, and time and again I was turned away whenever I attempted to enter an area restricted to members of Congress. Because I had won a special election following Sala's passing, I came to Congress alone, not as part of a freshman class.

I constantly had conversations that went something like this:

"I'm sorry, ma'am, this area is for members only."

"I am a member."

"Who are you?"

"Congresswoman Nancy Pelosi from California." I'd stand there while they looked up my name, made calls. I know they were just doing their jobs, but it happened quite frequently.

Finally I had a minor breakthrough. One day I was walking into a room, and a Capitol policeman said to me, "You can't go there, lady, that's for members only."

I said, for the umpteenth time, "But I am a member." This time, the policeman smiled and said, "Oh, if you're a member of Congress, you can go anywhere you want."

A few days later, I was on the floor of the House when one of the members went out the door to the Speaker's Lobby. I needed to see him, so I followed him as he proceeded through another doorway, an entrance framed in old-fashioned carved wood molding.

"You can't go there, you can't go there—stop!" a guard said.

"I can go anywhere I want," I declared. "I am a member of Congress!"

He looked sheepish. "Congresswoman, that's the men's room."

As Speaker, I am better recognized now inside and outside the Capitol. People want to say hello, though I have noticed that they will sometimes say the opposite of what they mean. In the excitement of the moment, they'll say, "Speaker Pelosi, you're my biggest fan!"

It happened to me again recently, only this time a man said, "You're my biggest fan! And you're even a bigger fan of my wife!" My ongoing favorite is "Speaker Pelosi, I'm your hero!" (What could I say except "Thank you very much"?) The most recent one was "Speaker Pelosi, I named my dog after you."

And leave it to a child to put it all in perspective. On the day before my swearing-in as Speaker, my grandson Ryan, then five years old, set our priorities straight.

We were being driven in a motorcade to Mass at Trinity College. My grandchildren were thrilled by the motorcycle escort. We thought Ryan was excited that his Mimi (my grandchildren's name for me) was becoming the first woman Speaker, when he announced, "This is what I'm going to be when I grow up."

His mom, my daughter, Jacqueline, asked, "You want to be Speaker of the House?"

"No," he replied. "I want to be a motorcycle policeman."

14

The Qualities You Need

I sometimes describe my job—as a Congresswoman, and as Whip, Leader, and Speaker of the House—as follows: You get up in the morning and eat nails for breakfast, you don a full suit of armor, and then you go to the floor, where you do battle.

And how can it not be a battle? We are deciding the issues that affect the lives and well-being of millions of people, and the political parties sometimes have diametrically opposing views.

Despite our heated debates even within our own party, I try to abide by the rule that burning bridges is unproductive. I came to Congress to build bridges, not burn them, and that's true of most of us who run for public office.

Every person in Congress was sent there by the American people, and we owe it to one another—and to all of our constituents—to treat one another in a civil way. In my swearing-in speech, I quoted Thomas Jefferson, who wrote, "Every difference of opinion is not a difference of principle."

In my speech I went on to say: "Respectful of the vision of our founders, the expectations of our people, and the great challenges we face, we have an obligation to reach beyond partisanship to serve all Americans. Let us all stand together to move our country forward, seeking common ground for the common good. We are from different parties but we serve one country."

The way I see it is that we are all colleagues and besides, you never know where your next vote might be coming from—whether on a committee or on the floor of the House—and that vote can make the difference between winning and losing. I frequently tell colleagues what I was told when I arrived here: "Never fight a fight as if it's your last one." Good advice, once again, from Lindy Boggs.

I've been in politics long enough to know that while there are eternal friendships—and I know that to be true, because I have them—there is no such thing as an eternal opponent. Someone who has been your adversary may be your friend down the road.

I always refer to coalition building in Congress as a giant kaleidoscope. With one turn of the dial, some of us will form a coalition for success. With another turn, a different group will come together on an issue.

Once you work with someone in a positive way on legislation, you have sown the seeds for cooperation in the future. A recent example of bipartisan cooperation was the economic stimulus package, passed early in 2008, where Democrats and Republicans approached the table with very different views, but after much discussion came away in agreement. It was urgent because we needed to get our economy moving.

But some people didn't think it was possible for us to reach that agreement, especially so quickly. I believe the openness that we had to one another's concerns helped us find common ground. And I succeeded with the Democratic goal, to give priority to the economic needs of middle- and lower-income people.

This is why you never draw a line in the sand, regardless of how irritated you are with your opponent. You have to leave an opening or a means for people to find their way back.

My brother Tommy has been the biggest influence on me politically. A very devout Catholic, he is the most principled and fairest politician I know, and I know many great politicians. He always advises me to put myself in my opponents' shoes and understand their point of view. He also says not to take politics personally and never let friendship leave your voice.

Tommy gave me valuable guidance that applies to many different fields besides government. "Know your budget and know your figures," he said. You can't make judgments unless you know how your idea is going to fit and how it's going to be paid for. Also, know the procedure. Not everyone does, and sometimes we all depend on a few people to know the procedure very well, and look to them for guidance. It's empowering to know the procedure yourself.

Congress is similar to any job in that you have to know the topic at hand. It's all about learning the subject and doing the work. This is especially important for a woman in any field dominated by men. If you know your stuff, it's very hard for them to diminish you.

Be able to defend your position with facts. While it's fine to use anecdotes to illustrate a position, they do not replace facts. We had a saying on the Appropriations Committee: "The plural of *anecdote* is not *data*." And when

I was on the Intelligence and the Ethics Committees, we were trained to consider the facts, the rules, and the law—nothing else.

While you have to know what you're talking about, you can't grandstand. When I first came to Congress, my friend and colleague, the extraordinarily talented and politically savvy George Miller, told me, "There's a free hedge-clipping service in Washington; you can put your head up just long enough so that you're making your mark for the people back home. But if you keep your head up too long, here comes that hedge clipper, and your head is gone."

In that competitive Congressional arena, it is important to listen carefully when you are counting votes. Nobody wants to say no to a colleague when you are running for a committee assignment or a leadership position. The first time I ran for a seat on the Appropriations Committee, I asked a senior member for his vote. I was complimented by his quick response: "Without even knowing who is in the race, I'm for you." I lost, and that person didn't vote for me. When I quoted his words back to him, he said, "That's right—I was for you not knowing who was in the race. Once I knew who was in the race I was for someone else."

Listen carefully to the words and the inflection, and

don't be misled by the response. "You'd be a great Whip" is not a yes. (It always comes back to knowing how to count the votes!)

To be successful in Congress, leaders must excel at three tasks: mastering the policy, understanding the politics, and knowing the people—most critically, how courageous they will be. It takes courage to go home and explain to your constituents that what is best for the district in the short term may not be in the best interests of the country in the long term.

Courage springs from the heart. I often say to my candidates, "Just show people a picture of what is in your heart." The voters know that what is in your heart is what you will have the courage to fight for.

I remember a speech given by David Henry Hwang, the author of *M. Butterfly,* when we were both receiving honorary degrees at the American Conservatory Theater in San Francisco. He said that many of the graduates had asked him what it was like to be successful on Broadway. He responded by saying that they should be wary of success. Failure is very silent, no one calls, and no one asks what you think. Success, on the other hand, is very noisy. Your phone rings constantly, and you're the center of attention. With all that noise of success, you sometimes can't hear what is in your heart, which is what got you there in the first place.

One of the best gifts I received from my parents was a passion to work for what I believe in. My passion is to make the future better for all children. That is why, when people ask me, "What makes you do this? What makes you work so hard?" I always have the same answer: "The one in five."

What motivates me every day in my political and personal life is the fact that one in five children in America lives in poverty. I think of them every morning when I wake up, about how they may have gone to sleep hungry the night before. And when my colleagues are having a frustrating day and they ask me, "Why should we do this?" I say, "Remember, it's for the one in five."

That is also why I began my swearing-in activities for Speaker with a Mass at Trinity College dedicated to the children of Darfur and Katrina. While standing in front of banners with photos of suffering children, Father Robert Drinan, S.J., and Rabbi David Saperstein challenged us to have the courage to help all of the children of the world.

We owe these children a better future and a chance to follow their dreams.

15

The Speaker and the President

I met George W. Bush for the first time when he was Governor of Texas and running for President. My introduction to him was through my daughter Alexandra, who was covering his campaign for NBC News.

Alexandra, who would go on to make a documentary film about the experience called *Journeys with George,* had been on the campaign trail with Governor Bush for nearly a year and a half when they came to Oakland, California, where he spoke at a rally.

While the reporters were filing their stories, Paul and I went to the hotel, with Paul Jr., to have lunch with Alexandra. And as we enjoyed our lunch, Governor Bush's aides came over to us and said to Alexandra, "The Governor would like to meet your parents."

Each time, I said the same thing: "That's so kind of the Governor, but we really came to see Alexandra, and we don't want to impose on him. We know he is busy."

Finally one aide, suspecting that I thought it would look like special treatment, said, "If anybody else's parents were here, he'd want to say hello to them, too."

We went in to see him. Laura Bush was there, too, and they were both very gracious. I knew the Governor had a sense of humor and wouldn't mind some honest give-and-take.

"Well, here I am in California," he said, grinning.

"And welcome to you, Governor," I replied. "But please understand we're doing everything possible to make sure you don't win—and everything possible to elect a Democratic Congress."

"Isn't this a great country?" he said, winking at his wife. And then, to us: "Hey, Alexandra's a great girl. A lot of fun to have around."

I hugged her. "Thank you," I said. "We think so, too."

That was 2000. Now, of course, he is President of the United States, and I am the Speaker of the House. Traditionally, the relationship is an important one. I knew that President Bush had a great deal of respect for the office of

the Speaker, because I could see at our leadership meet-
ings how he treated Dennis Hastert when he was Speaker.
And it was interesting to me that when I became Speaker,
I received the same level of respect from the President.

While we have a good personal rapport, we have major
disagreement on issues, especially on the Iraq War, and on
providing health care for millions more of America's children, which the President says we can't afford. The two
issues are related.

The story of the Bush Administration's war in Iraq is a
tangled tale, filled with endless misrepresentations. As the
senior Democrat on the Intelligence Committee at the
time of the Iraq vote, I said to the press when I voted "No"
on the war that the intelligence did not support the im-
minent threat the Administration was claiming.

And the press asked, "Are you calling the President
a liar?"

"I'm stating a fact," I replied.

That the intelligence differed from the Administration's
claims did not deter them from advancing more un-
founded threats and statements:

- "We don't want the smoking gun to be a mushroom
  cloud." —National Security Advisor Condoleezza
  Rice, September 8, 2002

- "From the standpoint of the Iraqi people, my belief is that we will, in fact, be greeted as liberators." —Vice President Dick Cheney, March 16, 2003
- "We are dealing with a country that can finance its own reconstruction and relatively soon." —Deputy Secretary of Defense Paul Wolfowitz, March 27, 2003

On March 19, 2003, on the feast of St. Joseph, I received a call from Condoleezza Rice. "The President asked me to inform you that in one hour we will initiate an attack on Iraq."

"Why now?" I asked. "We haven't exhausted all of the diplomatic and inspection remedies."

She replied that if we went into Iraq that night, it would "save lives." Though she couldn't speak fully on the phone, the reason later became known: The Administration thought they could kill Saddam Hussein that night.

But they were wrong on every score, whether describing the threat of weapons of mass destruction, the reception our troops would receive, or who would pay for the war.

As for the "mushroom cloud," inspections showed that there was no threat from weapons of mass destruction.

Instead of being "greeted as liberators" with rose petals, our troops were met with rocket-propelled grenades and roadside bombs.

Rather than Iraq "financ[ing] its own reconstruction and relatively soon," we are spending tens of billions of dollars on Iraq's infrastructure while the Iraqis build up a budget surplus.

As for going into Iraq that night to "save lives," the events of the past five years are well known to the American people. There have been over four thousand American deaths and well over a hundred thousand Iraqi deaths as of Easter weekend 2008, and still no end is in sight.

In May 2003, not long after President Bush had landed on the USS *Lincoln* and proclaimed the invasion of Iraq a success, we were at a leadership breakfast. "Mr. President," I said, "you have declared 'Mission Accomplished,' whatever that mission is. Now that we have shown our country's strength, I think it would be important to show its greatness."

"What do you mean?" he asked.

I said, "What I mean is that it's time for us to be magnanimous—to show the Islamic world that we respect them, and that we're not simply there for the oil, as so many people are saying. I don't know why we're there. But I do think it's time to reach out to the Islamic world because both the Arab elites and Arab street are watching to see what we do now."

President Bush looked impatient. "We don't have any

problem with the Arab elites and the Arab street," he said. "It's the French. They poisoned the well against us, and I'll never forget that."

That is the warped perspective of the President of the United States, and that is the judgment they expect us to follow.

The 2006 Congressional races, in which we regained control of Congress, should have been a message that a clear majority of voters wanted the United States out of Iraq. I had thought, mistakenly, that the President and the Republicans in Congress would respect the wishes of the American people. I had hoped we could find some common ground about how we could disengage from Iraq while at the same time agreeing on a vision for stability in the Middle East and refocusing our attention on the real War on Terror in Afghanistan.

But that is not what the President had in mind.

We sent a bill to his desk that called for the responsible, honorable, and safe redeployment of the troops out of Iraq, and he vetoed it. The message we got from him was, *I'm not doing anything differently.*

It was clear, then, that the President was fully committed to a war without end—a war that was predicated on false premises to begin with, with no plan or strategy, and without adequate training and equipment for the troops while cutting funding for veterans.

The war, and the President's blind eye to any disagreement, has caused great pain for our country, the loss of more than four thousand American lives being the most significant, but also the tens of thousands of injured, many of them permanently. I also worry about our troops' families—the divorces, the stress on relationships—because of the constant redeployments. Respectful of our troops and mindful of their sacrifices, the Democratic Congress voted the biggest increase in veterans' health benefits in the seventy-seven-year history of the Department of Veterans Affairs.

The Iraq War has dealt a severe blow to our reputation in the world. And we are now more, not less, vulnerable to terrorism, because the War in Iraq is turning our attention away from the real war on terrorism in Afghanistan. Meanwhile, the cost of the war to our military readiness is shameful and is now recognized, even by some of the President's advisors.

The vast amount of money, a projected $2–$3 trillion or more, is appalling. It is sad to think of what we could have done with that money—the opportunities lost. What initiatives could have been funded with the dollars we have spent on this war? What marvelous new ideas are delayed or may never see the light of day because there was no money to pay for them?

I said earlier that one of my other major areas of disagreement with the President was children's health care. A strong bipartisan majority in Congress voted for extending health care, called S-CHIP, to ten million more eligible children. The President said we couldn't afford it, and he vetoed our bipartisan bill. Forty days in Iraq could pay for ten million American children to be insured for one year.

Think of it—*forty days in Iraq could pay for ten million children getting health care in America for one year.*

And the President says we can't afford it.

We did get some Republican votes in the House, but not enough to override the President's veto. This never should have happened.

Following this defeat of S-CHIP, I started a series of conversations with scientists, health care professionals, grassroots activists, and business and labor leaders to frame the health issue in a new way. As the debate continues on how to make health care more accessible to the American people, we are also discussing access to what kind of care.

As one leading scientist told us bluntly, the American health care model is obsolete. It was as if we had said in the 1950s that the best way to fight polio was to build the best possible iron lung instead of also investing, as we did, in the research for a vaccine to rid the planet of polio.

It is time for a disruption. It is time for a new model, based on prevention and drastically increased investment in biomedical research. Do you know any family in America that has not been affected by cancer? Each year 550,000 people die in the United States from cancer. That's 1,500 Americans per day. We spend $5.5 billion per year on cancer research—that's less than what we spend in two weeks in Iraq.

Today there is cancer research that is promising but unfunded. This is immoral.

Imagine if we could divert some of the money spent in Iraq to health care. Think how much the American people would benefit. But President Bush says if we spend one dollar more than his budget request, he will veto the bill.

The White House contends that we can't afford one more dollar for basic biomedical research—but can spend more than 2 billion dollars a week in Iraq!

Let's end the war in Iraq and have a real war on cancer, diabetes, Alzheimer's, Parkinson's, heart disease, AIDS, and other illnesses.

President Bush took us into a war that took us into debt, which took us into recession. We need a New

Direction to create good-paying jobs here at home, by investing in innovation and science, by rebuilding America's infrastructure, by strengthening American families through education and health care, and by preserving our planet.

Since I've become Speaker, my flagship issue has been energy security and addressing the global climate crisis. We succeeded in passing a bipartisan energy bill that included the first increase in fuel efficiency standards in over thirty years. Energy independence is a national security, economic, environmental, health, and moral issue. This planet is God's creation, and we have a moral responsibility to preserve it.

The Speaker of the House I most admire is Tip O'Neill. Despite their differences, he was able to work in a bipartisan way with President Reagan to save Social Security. This was possible because they were both willing to listen and to compromise. I am certain that the American people and the Congress will give our new President the chance to take the country in a New Direction. I know that America can achieve true greatness when we work together to make certain that every voice in America is a voice that will be heard.

16

What Matters Most

No matter how swept up I get in my work in Washington, I have to make choices, just as all women do who are trying to balance home and work.

An example of this occurred several years ago, when our daughter Nancy Corinne was expecting a baby. At that same time, I was supposed to join a small group of members of Congress to accompany President Clinton to the Middle East. I was the senior Democrat on the Appropriations Foreign Operations Subcommittee, and the trip was part of a major Clinton foreign policy initiative. Being part of the delegation was an honor and a recognition of my role in foreign affairs.

I studied my calendar. If everything went just right, I

could go and still be back by Nancy Corinne's due date.

On the morning I was to leave, I was to be picked up by the Air Force from my Washington apartment at 5:30 A.M. to go to Andrews Air Force Base. I packed my bag the night before and went to sleep.

And then the phone rang.

At first I thought I had slept through the alarm. But it wasn't the Air Force. It was Paul, calling from San Francisco. He said, "You have a choice. You can go to the Middle East, or you can go to Arizona and watch your new grandchild arrive."

Nancy Corinne was in labor, a week early. And my choice was clear. "I'm all packed," I said.

Every woman I know would have made the same decision. I raced to the airport and got on the first plane to Phoenix, prayed for my daughter and the baby through the whole four-hour flight, hurried off the plane, and asked the taxi driver to please take the quickest route to the hospital. I dashed off the elevator at the hospital and raced down the hall to the delivery room—which Nancy Corinne and her brand-new baby were just leaving. The elated new father, Jeff Prowda, was wheeling them to their room, where "Pop"—grandfather Paul Pelosi, who had gotten there ahead of me—was waiting for them.

"What did we have?" I asked breathlessly.

"It's a girl." Our Madeleine had arrived in the world—and she was absolutely beautiful.

And do you know what? Going there was not a hard decision. Not even close.

Having been a young mother to five little ones, I know that you don't want to miss the big moments. You can't get them back. And I wasn't about to miss the sight of my daughter holding her newborn daughter in her arms.

Madeleine has grown into a poised little girl. The day before my swearing-in ceremony as Speaker, she made a few remarks of her own, which she gave during a tea held in honor of Ann Richards, the late Governor of Texas, and all of the other women who had made my Speakership possible.

"My Mimi is going to be the first woman Speaker of the House," Madeleine said with all of the earnestness of an eight-year-old. "Because Mimi got this job, I think more women will get jobs like hers, which is *great*."

Madeleine wrote her own speech, and her words inspired everyone present, including, of course, her proud Mimi.

The next day, when I was sworn in as Speaker, there were many children present, as it is customary for members of Congress to bring their families to swearing-in ceremonies at the Capitol. Seeing the excited children in the chamber, I broke protocol by inviting *all* of the children to join my grandchildren at the podium.

The moment I took the Speaker's gavel was, as I've said, an historic moment for the Congress as well as for the women of America. But it was also a victory for America's children and their future. For the first time in history, the Speaker opened the House by saying, "For *all* of America's children, the House will be in order."

I consider my involvement in politics as an extension of my role as a mom.

More than anything else, I am a wife, mother, and grandmother. If I had never done anything in addition to being a mother to our five children, and now a grandmother, I would consider my life a happy success.

Hearing Nancy Corinne's laugh, listening to Christine's voice, seeing Jacqueline's smile, appreciating Paul Jr.'s energy, and enjoying Alexandra's humor have been the joys of my life. Five great children from the same family, same environment—but five completely different people.

When Nancy Corinne was born, my mother called her "Little Pink Lady" because of her rosy cheeks. A few years later my father started calling her "Miss Boss," for taking charge of the younger babies when she was two and a half years old. On our first night in California, she walked into Nana's house and announced—she was then four—that no one should kiss the baby on the lips and everyone should wash their hands before touching him. "Not on the lips" was her mantra.

When Paul and I brought Alexandra home from the hospital, it was the week of Nancy Corinne's sixth birthday. She was standing at the curb. When the car door opened, she said with arms outstretched, "Hand her over."

As they got older, Nancy Corinne would supervise the children's grocery shopping. Sometimes she allowed forbidden sugary cereals to be sneaked into our home, winning the favor of her siblings.

She not only is a wonderful mother and wife to Jeff but also was a loving and attentive granddaughter to Nana and my parents. She loves taking care of her family and friends. No wonder she is in the hospitality business.

Nancy Corinne and Jeff have two children—Alexander, our firstborn grandchild, and Madeleine. Alexander, who is eleven, loves sports, worries about the poor, and is protective of Madeleine, who rules the roost. Madeleine, now nine, loves school and soccer and says that her life is perfect except that it is "petless."

Christine, our second daughter, fulfilled my mother's dream when she passed the California bar exam. Christine has had her nose in a book almost from birth. Paul said at her wedding that she was the only one of our children who had to be told, "Put that book down and go outside and play." One day I called out to her to be careful crossing the street, and she replied that she was busy "thinking of all of the wonderful rectangles in the world."

Christine was always the one most interested in politics. Even as a little girl, on our grocery-shopping trips, she would make sure that nothing we were buying would exploit workers. We, of course, didn't buy California grapes because the farm workers were on strike, but when Christine's activism extended to her siblings' favorite cookies, the other children rebelled and said, "Mom promised politics wouldn't interfere with our lives." Two of Christine's loves, books and politics, came together in the publication of her own book, *Campaign Boot Camp*.

Christine's husband, Peter, and his son, Octavio, share her passion for sports. She knows every sports statistic and even moved across the street from AT&T Park to be close to the Giants' games.

Jacqueline, our third daughter, was called "Little French Pastry" by my father because she was so sweet. Sensitive and kind, Jacqueline always asked caring questions. When the children were little, we visited the replica of Sir Francis Drake's *Golden Hind* and everyone was asking questions:

How big is the ship? How fast did it sail? How long did it take to get from England to America?

Jacqueline, meanwhile, was off talking to the crew, asking if they liked being at sea, whether they have families back home, and what they wanted to do next. Jacqueline is dedicated to working with children, especially those with special needs, and started Art Mix, her creative arts learning center in Houston.

Jacqueline and her husband, Michael, have three sons—Liam, Sean, and Ryan—and a dog, Bella. All of the Kenneally boys are U2 fans. Liam, eleven, is the leader of the pack—he loves school, sports, and art. Sean, nine, is in constant Bono mode and has memorized all of U2's recordings since he was three. Ryan, six, is our motorcycle policeman—or any other first responder. They have all met Bono on more than one occasion and think that they, Bono, and Edge are good friends. U2's "Elevation" is one of their favorite songs, and working with Bono on global poverty and AIDS issues has certainly elevated me in my grandchildren's eyes.

Our fourth child and only son, Paul Jr., is tall and very athletic. He was on the national championship track team in college. Everyone says he looks just like his father. But I say he is a combination because he reminds me of my brothers. Paul got his BA, MBA, and law degree from Georgetown, and I enjoyed having him in Washington for eight years. His credentials also include making the Thanksgiving turkey and putting the lights on the Christmas tree.

Although he escaped his sisters and their girlfriends to go away to Episcopal High School, Paul Jr. has always been a good brother. He and Alexandra were especially close growing up. In early family photos, he always seems to have his hand on her shoulder so that she won't fall. He is a wonderful uncle and godfather. I have learned a lot by listening to him talk with great knowledge and enthusiasm about the environment and the global climate crisis. Paul is our world traveler, but he always comes home to San Francisco.

Alexandra first got involved in the media when she was in high school, sneaking out at night to do the graveyard shift at the University of San Francisco radio station. Paul and I, of course, did not know this until years later, but I still tremble at the thought. She only applied to Loyola Marymount for college because they had the best college radio station in the nation. She received her master's degree at the Annenberg School at USC where, I think, she finally went to class.

At Nana's funeral her prayer of the faithful was "for all

mothers to be like Nana and have enough love in their hearts to meet the needs of their children."

Funny, wry, and madly in love with her husband, Michiel, and their two small sons, Alexandra is the only one of our children born in San Francisco, though today she says she is a confirmed New Yorker. Her adorable little boys, Paulie and Thomas, are nineteen months and six months, respectively, and both already are rocking to the music.

When I was first elected to the Democratic leadership, I received messages of congratulations from women and girls around the world. What was interesting to me was the large number of good wishes I also received from fathers of daughters, who saw my success as opening new opportunities for girls. I appreciated the sentiment because of the special relationship Paul always had with our daughters.

One of my favorite messages was written on stationery headed with an Eleanor Roosevelt quote: "The future belongs to those who believe in the beauty of their dreams." What a wonderful sentiment! And what a wonderful and exhilarating time to be a woman in America, where there are no limits to our futures, no limit to the beauty of our dreams.

As long as we recognize the power within us, we will continue to have choices, and we will continue to lead.

The source of that power can be the other people who guide us. It can come from the knowledge that courageous women throughout history paved the way for us. It can come from our roots and our families, which give us strength. And it must come from within ourselves—from our faith, our accomplishments, and our values.

Know your power.

When you do, others will know your power, too.

INDEX

Afghanistan, 160, 161

Agnos, Art, 89

Alioto, Joseph, 55–56, 64

Anthony, Susan B., 124

Art Mix, 171

Aung San Suu Kyi, 97

Bailey, John M., 126

Baltimore, Maryland, 10, 57

    Albemarle Street, 26, 81, 82

    Enoch Pratt Free Library, 56

    Fifth Regiment Armory, 12

    Jerry Brown campaign in, 61

    Little Italy, 11, 23

    St. Leo's Church, 11

    Thomas D'Alesandro, Jr., 10, 12, 14, 21, 88

    Thomas D'Alesandro III, 41–42, 57

Becerra, Xavier, 132

Belvedere, California, 53

Bergson Group, 97

Boehner, John, 8

Boggs, Hale, 125

Boggs, Lindy, 125, 127, 148

Bonior, David, 104

Bono, 171

Boxer, Barbara, 111, 137, 142, 143

Brown, Jerry, 61–63

Brown, Michael "Brownie," 116–17

Brown, Willie, 66

Bryan, William Jennings, 12

Burma, 97

Burton, John, 73, 75, 76, 80

Burton, Phillip, 5, 70, 71, 110

Burton, Sala, 5–7, 68, 69, 70, 71, 73, 74, 75, 99, 143

Bush, George H. W., 93–94, 96, 126

Bush, George W., 95, 112–13, 114, 115–16, 117, 155–63

Bush, Laura, 156

California Democratic Party, 64–65

Campaign Boot Camp (C. Pelosi), 170

Capitol Building, Washington, DC, 9–10

Carter, Jimmy, 63

Chavez, Cesar, 83

Cheney, Dick, 158

Chicago, Illinois, 42

China, 92–96
    Pelosi trip, 94–95, 96
    Tiananmen Square, 92–94, 98
    Tibet issue, 95–96, 97
    2008 Olympics, 98

Christensen, Clayton, 133

Civil Rights Movement, 96

Clinton, Bill, 97, 126, 165

Clyburn, Jim, 132

Convent of the Sacred Heart, 19, 106

Cullinane, John, 112

Cuomo, Mario, 66, 73

Dalai Lama, 95

D'Alesandro, Franklin Roosevelt, 57, 114

D'Alesandro, Hector, 14, 57

D'Alesandro, Joseph "Joey," 14

D'Alesandro, Margie, 42, 90

D'Alesandro, Nancy Lombardi, 10–13, 17–18, 22–23, 25–27, 31, 37, 38

D'Alesandro, Nicholas, 57

D'Alesandro, Nicholas (Little Nicky), 25

D'Alesandro, Thomas, III, 22, 25, 40–42, 55, 57, 63, 81–82, 150

D'Alesandro, Thomas, Jr., 9–13, 18, 21, 22, 25, 28–30, 31, 32, 37, 40, 41–42, 43, 80–82, 83, 88, 97, 114

Daley, Richard, 42

Darfur, 97–98, 153

Daschle, Tom, 111

Davis, Susan, 103

DeLauro, Rosa, 101, 132

Dellums, Ron, 136

Democratic Congressional Campaign Committee (DCCC), 102

Democratic National Committee Chair, 69–70, 72, 78, 126

Democratic National Convention
    Chicago, Illinois (1968), 41–42
    Los Angeles, California (1960), 29, 45
    New York City (1976), 64
    San Francisco (1984), 66–67, 80

Dingell, John, 132

Dodd, Christopher, 126

Dodd, Martha, 32

Dodd, Thomas, 33

Drinan, Father Robert, S.J., 153

Economic stimulus package, 149

Edwards, Don, 138

Emanuel, Rahm, 26, 27., 118, 132

Episcopal High School, 172

Equal Rights Amendment, 138

Eshoo, Anna, 98

Family and Medical Leave Act, 126

Feinstein, Dianne, 66, 111

Ferraro, Geraldine, 66–67

Foley, Tom, 100

Francis of Assisi, Saint, 85

Frank, Barney, 91–92

Gandhi, Mohandas, 96

Ganz, Marshall, 83

Georgetown University, 20, 35, 36, 39, 172

Gephardt, Dick, 102–105

Getty, Gordon and Ann, 53

Golden Gate Recreational Area (GGNRA), 110

Goodall, Jane, 54

Guggenhime family, 53

Hambrecht, Sally and Bill, 53

Harman, Jane, 103

Hart, Gary, 66

Harvey, Charlene, 110

Harvey, Jim, 110

Hastert, Dennis, 157

Hepburn, Nancy, 15

HIV/AIDS, 85, 86–87, 89–90, 161, 169

 NAMES Quilt, 87–89

Honda, Mike, 103

House Resolution 1, 132

Hoyer, Steny, 132

Huerta, Dolores, 83

Humphrey, Hubert, 41-42

Hurricane Katrina, 116, 153

Hussein, Saddam, 158

Hwang, David Henry, 152

ILWU (International Longshore and Warehouse Union), 8

Innovator's Dilemma, The and *The Innovator's Solution* (Christensen), 133

Institute of Notre Dame (I.N.D.), Baltimore, Maryland, 24, 27

Iraq War, 157–62, 163

Jefferson, Thomas, 148

Johnson, Lyndon B., 41, 42

Jones, Ben, 94

Jones, Cleve, 89, 90, 91

Joseph, Saint, 158

Journeys with George (film), 155

Kenneally, Liam, 171

Kenneally, Michael, 171

Kenneally, Ryan, 144–45, 171

Kenneally, Sean, 171

Kennedy, John F., 27–30, 41

Kennedy, Robert F., 41

Kennelly, Barbara, 126, 137

Khartoum, 98

King, Martin Luther, Jr., 38, 41, 96, 133

Lantos, Tom, 98

Larson, John, 132

Lauter, Bob and Naomi, 53

Leakey, Richard, 54

Lewis, John, 38

Lofgren, Zoe, 103

Los Angeles, California, 29

Lowey, Nita, 101

Loyola Marymount, 172

L.S.B. Leakey Foundation, 54

Lynett, Celia, 32

Malvern Prep, 39

March on Washington for Jobs and Freedom, 38

Markey, Ed, 112

McCarthy, Leo, 62, 63, 65, 73, 89

McGarraghy, Mary Catherine, 32

McGeehan, Sally, 15

McKeldin, Theodore Roosevelt, 14

Meyer, Amy, 110

Meyer, Denny, 35

Mikulski, Barbara, 24

Miller, George, 111, 132, 151

Miller, John, 94

Mindszenty, Jozsef, 26

Mink, Patsy, 126

Mitchell, George, 73

Mondale, Walter, 66, 67

Mott, Lucretia, 124

Murray, Rita, 32, 35

Murtha, Jack, 111

National Institutes of Health, 101

"New Direction—Six for '06," 118, 119, 132

Newsom, Gavin, 85

New York City, 39

    Democratic National Convention (1976), 64

9/11 Commission Recommendations, 132

Nixon, Richard, 49

Obey, David, 101

Ocean City, Maryland, 15–16

O'Neill, Tip, 164

Partnership for America's Future, 112

Paul, Alice, 124

Pawtucket, Rhode Island, 10

Pelosi, Alexandra, 50, 72–73, 141–42, 155–56, 168, 169, 172–73

Pelosi, Christine, 6, 20, 39, 47, 50, 79, 127, 168, 169–70

Pelosi, Corinne Bianchi "Nana," 46, 47–48, 49, 50, 77, 83, 169, 173

Pelosi, David, 46, 62

Pelosi, Jacqueline, 19–20, 39, 47, 51,
  52, 145, 168, 170–71
Pelosi, John, 46
Pelosi, Nancy Corinne, 6, 39, 47, 50,
  165, 166, 168–69
Pelosi, Paul, 6, 16, 19, 34, 35–39, 42,
  45–47, 48–49, 51–52, 62, 69, 71,
  75–76, 78, 79, 83, 106–7, 155,
  166, 169, 171, 173
Pelosi, Paul, Jr., 19-20, 45, 47, 155,
  168, 171–72
Pelosi, Ronald, 47, 62
Perkins, Frances, 114
Piracci, Susie, 90
Prowda, Alexander, 169
Prowda, Jeff, 166, 169
Prowda, Madeleine, 167, 169

Quigley, Carroll, 36

Rangel, Charlie, 132
Reagan, Ronald, 164
Regula, Ralph, 111
Reid, Harry, 112, 114–16
Reilly, Clint, 74
Ribicoff, Abraham, 42
Rice, Condoleezza, 157, 158
Richards, Ann, 167
Roosevelt, Eleanor, 173
Roosevelt, Franklin D., 10, 97
Rosenblatt, Toby, 111
Ross, Fred Jr., 83
Ross, Mike, 104

Russo, Marty, 138
Rwanda, 97

St. Ignatius High School, 62
St. Vincent de Paul Catholic
  Church, 46
San Francisco, 29, 43, 45, 47
  American Conservatory
    Theater, 152
  Chinatown, 92
  Democratic National Convention
    (1984), 66
  Julius Kahn Playground,
    Presidio, 53
  Library Commission, 56–57
  Pelosi house, Presidio Terrace,
    52–53, 76
  Presidio (Golden Gate National
    Recreational Area), 109–11, 119
Saperstein, Rabbi David, 153
Satyagraha, 96
Schiff, Adam, 103
S-CHIP, 162
Schroeder, Pat, 126, 136, 137
Seeley, J. R., 33
Shorenstein, Walter, 66
Shriver, Sargent, 36
Sisters of Notre Dame de Namur, 33
Sklar, Barbara and Dick, 53
Slaughter, Louise, 132
Social Security, 113–16, 164
Solis, Hilda, 103
Stanton, Elizabeth Cady, 124

Stark, Pete, 138

Starr, Kevin, 56

Starr, Sheila, 56

Stevenson, Adlai, 27

Sudan, 98

Teresa, Mother, 98

Thompson, Mike, 103

Tibet, 95–96, 97, 98

Title IX Amendment to Education
    Act, 126

Town School for Boys, 19, 106

Trinity College, Washington DC, 31,
    126, 153

UFW (United Farm Workers), 83

United Nations Association of
    Maryland, 27

University of San Francisco, 172

University of Southern
    California, 172

U. S. Congress
    AIDS subcommittee, 101
    Appropriations Committee, 101,
        123, 150, 151
    Armed Services Committee, 136
    Banking Committee, 101
    Ethics Committee, 101, 151
    Foreign Operations
        Committee, 165
    freshmen, 134–35
    Intelligence Committee, 101, 123,
        157

Labor, Health, and Human
    Services Committee, 101

Majority Leader, 105, 132

Minority Leader, 102

Nancy Pelosi wins seat, 7, 83–84

Rules Committee, 132

Speaker of the House, 1, 2, 8, 26,
    100–101, 126–27, 131–32, 133,
    135, 139, 143–45, 147, 153,
    155–64, 167–68

Thomas D'Alesandro in, 10, 12

Whip, 100, 102, 104–5, 123–24,
    132, 147, 151

women in, 124–25, 135

U. S. Department of Veterans
    Affairs, 161

USS *Lincoln*, 159

U2, 171

Van Hollen, Chris, 132

Venetoulis, Ted, 63

Walker, Kay Kimpton, 53

War on Terror, 160

Wayburn, Ed, 110

Wilson, Woodrow, 12

Wolff, Brian, 103

Wolfington, Alicia Usera, 39

Wolfington, Vince, 39

Wolfowitz, Paul, 158

Woods, Kay and Frank, 53

Wright, Jim, 88

Wyman, Roz, 66

DATE DUE

JUL -- 2008